On
Managing
Risk

HBR's 10 Must Reads series is the definitive collection of ideas and best practices for aspiring and experienced leaders alike. These books offer essential reading selected from the pages of *Harvard Business Review* on topics critical to the success of every manager.

Titles include:

On
Managing
Risk

HARVARD BUSINESS REVIEW PRESS
Boston, Massachusetts

Library of Congress Cataloging-in-Publication Data

Title: HBR's 10 must reads on managing risk / Harvard Business Review.
Other titles: Harvard Business Review's ten must reads on managing risk |
    HBR's 10 must reads (Series)
Description: Boston, Massachusetts : Harvard Business Review Press, [2020]
    | Series: HBR's 10 must reads series | Includes index.
Identifiers: LCCN 2019054430 (print) | LCCN 2019054431 (ebook) | ISBN
    9781633698864 (paperback) | ISBN 9781633698871 (ebook)
Subjects: LCSH: Risk management. | Success in business.
Classification: LCC HD61 .H353 2020 (print) | LCC HD61 (ebook) | DDC
    658.15/5—dc23
LC record available at https://lccn.loc.gov/2019054430
LC ebook record available at https://lccn.loc.gov/2019054431

ISBN: 978-1-63369-886-4
eISBN: 978-1-63369-887-1

Contents

On
Managing
Risk

Managing Risks

A New Framework. *by Robert S. Kaplan and Anette Mikes*

WHEN TONY HAYWARD BECAME CEO OF BP, in 2007, he vowed to make safety his top priority. Among the new rules he instituted were the requirements that all employees use lids on coffee cups while walking and refrain from texting while driving. Three years later, on Hayward's watch, the Deepwater Horizon oil rig exploded in the Gulf of Mexico, causing one of the worst man-made disasters in history. A U.S. investigation commission attributed the disaster to management failures that crippled "the ability of individuals involved to identify the risks they faced and to properly evaluate, communicate, and address them."

Hayward's story reflects a common problem. Despite all the rhetoric and money invested in it, risk management is too often treated as a compliance issue that can be solved by drawing up lots of rules and making sure that all employees follow them. Many such rules, of course, are sensible and do reduce some risks that could severely damage a company. But rules-based risk management will not diminish either the likelihood or the impact of a disaster such as Deepwater Horizon, just as it did not prevent the failure of many financial institutions during the 2007–2008 credit crisis.

Understanding the three categories of risk

The risks that companies face fall into three categories, each of which requires a different risk-management approach. Preventable risks, arising from within an organization, are monitored and controlled through rules, values, and standard compliance tools. In contrast, strategy risks and external risks require distinct processes that encourage managers to openly discuss risks and find cost-effective ways to reduce the likelihood of risk events or mitigate their consequences.

Category 1: Preventable risks	Category 2: Strategy risks	Category 3: External risks
Risks arising from within the company that generate no strategic benefits	Risks taken for superior strategic returns	External, uncontrollable risks
Risk mitigation objective		
Avoid or eliminate occurrence cost-effectively	Reduce likelihood and impact cost-effectively	Reduce impact cost effectively should a risk event occur
Control model		
Integrated culture-and-compliance model: Develop mission statement; values and belief systems; rules and boundary systems; standard operating procedures; internal controls and internal audit	Interactive discussions about risks to strategic objectives drawing on tools such as: • Maps of likelihood and impact of identified risks • Key risk indicator (KRI) scorecards Resource allocation to mitigate critical risk events	"Envisioning" risks through: • Tail-risk assessments and stress testing • Scenario planning • War-gaming
Role of risk-management staff function		
Coordinates, oversees, and revises specific risk controls with internal audit function	Runs risk workshops and risk review meetings Helps develop portfolio of risk initiatives and their funding Acts as devil's advocates	Runs stress-testing, scenario-planning, and war-gaming exercises with management team Acts as devil's advocates
Relationship of the risk-management function to business units		
Acts as independent overseers	Acts as independent facilitators, independent experts, or embedded experts	Complements strategy team or serves as independent facilitators of "envisioning" exercises

Idea in Brief

For all the rhetoric about its importance and the money invested in it, risk management is too often treated as a compliance issue.

A rules-based risk-management system may work well to align values and control employee behavior, but it is unsuitable for managing risks inherent in a company's strategic choices or the risks posed by major disruptions or changes in the external environment. Those types of risk require systems aimed at generating discussion and debate.

For strategy risks, companies must tailor approaches to the scope of the risks involved and their rate of change. Though the risk-management functions may vary from company to company, all such efforts must be anchored in corporate strategic-planning processes.

To manage major external risks outside the company's control, companies can call on tools such as war-gaming and scenario analysis. The choice of approach depends on the immediacy of the potential risk's impact and whether it arises from geopolitical, environmental, economic, or competitive changes.

In this article, we present a new categorization of risk that allows executives to tell which risks can be managed through a rules-based model and which require alternative approaches. We examine the individual and organizational challenges inherent in generating open, constructive discussions about managing the risks related to strategic choices and argue that companies need to anchor these discussions in their strategy formulation and implementation processes. We conclude by looking at how organizations can identify and prepare for nonpreventable risks that arise externally to their strategy and operations.

Managing Risk: Rules or Dialogue?

The first step in creating an effective risk-management system is to understand the qualitative distinctions among the types of risks that organizations face. Our field research shows that risks fall into one of three categories. Risk events from any category can be fatal to a company's strategy and even to its survival.

Identifying and Managing Preventable Risks

COMPANIES CANNOT ANTICIPATE EVERY CIRCUMSTANCE or conflict of interest that an employee might encounter.

Thus, the first line of defense against preventable risk events is to provide guidelines clarifying the company's goals and values.

The Mission

A well-crafted mission statement articulates the organization's fundamental purpose, serving as a "true north" for all employees to follow. The first sentence of Johnson & Johnson's renowned credo, for instance, states, "We believe our first responsibility is to the doctors, nurses and patients, to mothers and fathers, and all others who use our products and services," making clear to all employees whose interests should take precedence in any situation. Mission statements should be communicated to and understood by all employees.

The Values

Companies should articulate the values that guide employee behavior toward principal stakeholders, including customers, suppliers, fellow employees, communities, and shareholders. Clear value statements help employees avoid violating the company's standards and putting its reputation and assets at risk.

Category I: Preventable risks

These are internal risks, arising from within the organization, that are controllable and ought to be eliminated or avoided. Examples are the risks from employees' and managers' unauthorized, illegal, unethical, incorrect, or inappropriate actions and the risks from breakdowns in routine operational processes. To be sure, companies should have a zone of tolerance for defects or errors that would not cause severe damage to the enterprise and for which achieving complete avoidance would be too costly. But in general, companies should seek to eliminate these risks since they get no strategic benefits from taking them on. A rogue trader or an employee bribing a local official may produce some short-term profits for the firm, but over time such actions will diminish the company's value.

The Boundaries

A strong corporate culture clarifies what is not allowed. An explicit definition of boundaries is an effective way to control actions. Consider that nine of the Ten Commandments and nine of the first 10 amendments to the U.S. Constitution (commonly known as the Bill of Rights) are written in negative terms. Companies need corporate codes of business conduct that prescribe behaviors relating to conflicts of interest, antitrust issues, trade secrets and confidential information, bribery, discrimination, and harassment.

Of course, clearly articulated statements of mission, values, and boundaries don't in themselves ensure good behavior. To counter the day-to-day pressures of organizational life, top managers must serve as role models and demonstrate that they mean what they say. Companies must institute strong internal control systems, such as the segregation of duties and an active whistle-blowing program, to reduce not only misbehavior but also temptation. A capable and independent internal audit department tasked with continually checking employees' compliance with internal controls and standard operating processes also will deter employees from violating company procedures and policies and can detect violations when they do occur.

This risk category is best managed through active prevention: monitoring operational processes and guiding people's behaviors and decisions toward desired norms. Since considerable literature already exists on the rules-based compliance approach, we refer interested readers to the sidebar "Identifying and Managing Preventable Risks" in lieu of a full discussion of best practices here.

Category II: Strategy risks

A company voluntarily accepts some risk in order to generate superior returns from its strategy. A bank assumes credit risk, for example, when it lends money; many companies take on risks through their research and development activities.

Strategy risks are quite different from preventable risks because they are not inherently undesirable. A strategy with high expected returns generally requires the company to take on significant risks, and managing those risks is a key driver in capturing the potential gains. BP accepted the high risks of drilling several miles below the surface of the Gulf of Mexico because of the high value of the oil and gas it hoped to extract.

Strategy risks cannot be managed through a rules-based control model. Instead, you need a risk-management system designed to reduce the probability that the assumed risks actually materialize and to improve the company's ability to manage or contain the risk events should they occur. Such a system would not stop companies from undertaking risky ventures; to the contrary, it would enable companies to take on higher-risk, higher-reward ventures than could competitors with less effective risk management.

Category III: External risks

Some risks arise from events outside the company and are beyond its influence or control. Sources of these risks include natural and political disasters and major macroeconomic shifts. External risks require yet another approach. Because companies cannot prevent such events from occurring, their management must focus on identification (they tend to be obvious in hindsight) and mitigation of their impact.

Companies should tailor their risk-management processes to these different categories. While a compliance-based approach is effective for managing preventable risks, it is wholly inadequate for strategy risks or external risks, which require a fundamentally different approach based on open and explicit risk discussions. That, however, is easier said than done; extensive behavioral and organizational research has shown that individuals have strong cognitive biases that discourage them from thinking about and discussing risk until it's too late.

Why Risk Is Hard to Talk About

Multiple studies have found that people overestimate their ability to influence events that, in fact, are heavily determined by chance. We tend to be *overconfident* about the accuracy of our forecasts and risk assessments and far too narrow in our assessment of the range of outcomes that may occur.

We also *anchor our estimates* to readily available evidence despite the known danger of making linear extrapolations from recent history to a highly uncertain and variable future. We often compound this problem with a *confirmation bias,* which drives us to favor information that supports our positions (typically successes) and suppress information that contradicts them (typically failures). When events depart from our expectations, we tend to *escalate commitment,* irrationally directing even more resources to our failed course of action—throwing good money after bad.

Organizational biases also inhibit our ability to discuss risk and failure. In particular, teams facing uncertain conditions often engage in *groupthink*: Once a course of action has gathered support within a group, those not yet on board tend to suppress their objections—however valid—and fall in line. Groupthink is especially likely if the team is led by an overbearing or overconfident manager who wants to minimize conflict, delay, and challenges to his or her authority.

Collectively, these individual and organizational biases explain why so many companies overlook or misread ambiguous threats. Rather than mitigating risk, firms actually incubate risk through the *normalization of deviance,* as they learn to tolerate apparently minor failures and defects and treat early warning signals as false alarms rather than alerts to imminent danger.

Effective risk-management processes must counteract those biases. "Risk mitigation is painful, not a natural act for humans to perform," says Gentry Lee, the chief systems engineer at Jet Propulsion Laboratory (JPL), a division of the U.S. National Aeronautics and Space Administration. The rocket scientists on JPL project teams are top graduates from elite universities, many of whom have never experienced failure at school or work. Lee's biggest challenge in establishing a new risk culture at JPL was to get project teams to feel comfortable thinking and talking about what could go wrong with their excellent designs.

Rules about what to do and what not to do won't help here. In fact, they usually have the opposite effect, encouraging a checklist mentality that inhibits challenge and discussion. Managing strategy risks and external risks requires very different approaches. We start by examining how to identify and mitigate strategy risks.

Managing Strategy Risks

Over the past 10 years of study, we've come across three distinct approaches to managing strategy risks. Which model is appropriate for a given firm depends largely on the context in which an organization operates. Each approach requires quite different structures and roles for a risk-management function, but all three encourage employees to challenge existing assumptions and debate risk information. Our finding that "one size does not fit all" runs counter to the efforts of regulatory authorities and professional associations to standardize the function.

Independent experts

Some organizations—particularly those like JPL that push the envelope of technological innovation—face high intrinsic risk as they pursue long, complex, and expensive product-development projects. But since much of the risk arises from coping with known laws of nature, the risk changes slowly over time. For these organizations, risk management can be handled at the project level.

JPL, for example, has established a risk review board made up of independent technical experts whose role is to challenge project engineers' design, risk-assessment, and risk-mitigation decisions. The experts ensure that evaluations of risk take place periodically throughout the product-development cycle. Because the risks are relatively unchanging, the review board needs to meet only once or twice a year, with the project leader and the head of the review board meeting quarterly.

The risk review board meetings are intense, creating what Gentry Lee calls "a culture of intellectual confrontation." As board member Chris Lewicki says, "We tear each other apart, throwing stones and giving very critical commentary about everything that's going on." In the process, project engineers see their work from another perspective. "It lifts their noses away from the grindstone," Lewicki adds.

The meetings, both constructive and confrontational, are not intended to inhibit the project team from pursuing highly ambitious missions and designs. But they force engineers to think in advance about how they will describe and defend their design decisions and whether they have sufficiently considered likely failures and defects. The board members, acting as devil's advocates, counterbalance the engineers' natural overconfidence, helping to avoid escalation of commitment to projects with unacceptable levels of risk.

At JPL, the risk review board not only promotes vigorous debate about project risks but also has authority over budgets. The board establishes cost and time reserves to be set aside for each project component according to its degree of innovativeness. A simple extension from a prior mission would require a 10% to 20% financial reserve, for instance, whereas an entirely new component that had yet to work on Earth—much less on an unexplored planet—could require a 50% to 75% contingency. The reserves ensure that when problems inevitably arise, the project team has access to the money and time needed to resolve them without jeopardizing the launch date. JPL takes the estimates seriously; projects have been deferred or canceled if funds were insufficient to cover recommended reserves.

Facilitators
Many organizations, such as traditional energy and water utilities, operate in stable technological and market environments, with relatively predictable customer demand. In these situations risks stem largely from seemingly unrelated operational choices across a complex organization that accumulate gradually and can remain hidden for a long time.

Since no single staff group has the knowledge to perform operational-level risk management across diverse functions, firms may deploy a relatively small central risk-management group that collects information from operating managers. This increases managers' awareness of the risks that have been taken on across the organization and provides decision makers with a full picture of the company's risk profile.

We observed this model in action at Hydro One, the Canadian electricity company. Chief risk officer John Fraser, with the explicit backing of the CEO, runs dozens of workshops each year at which employees from all levels and functions identify and rank the principal risks they see to the company's strategic objectives. Employees use an anonymous voting technology to rate each risk, on a scale of 1 to 5, in terms of its impact, the likelihood of occurrence, and the strength of existing controls. The rankings are discussed in the workshops, and employees are empowered to voice and debate their risk perceptions. The group ultimately develops a consensus view that gets recorded on a visual risk map, recommends action plans, and designates an "owner" for each major risk.

Hydro One strengthens accountability by linking capital allocation and budgeting decisions to identified risks. The corporate-level capital-planning process allocates hundreds of millions of dollars, principally to projects that reduce risk effectively and efficiently. The risk group draws upon technical experts to challenge line engineers' investment plans and risk assessments and to provide independent expert oversight to the resource allocation process. At the annual capital allocation meeting, line managers have to defend their proposals in front of their peers and top executives. Managers want their projects to attract funding in the risk-based capital planning process, so they learn to overcome their bias to hide or minimize the risks in their areas of accountability.

Embedded experts

The financial services industry poses a unique challenge because of the volatile dynamics of asset markets and the potential impact of decisions made by decentralized traders and investment managers. An investment bank's risk profile can change dramatically with a single deal or major market movement. For such companies, risk management requires embedded experts within the organization to continuously monitor and influence the business's risk profile, working side by side with the line managers whose activities are generating new ideas, innovation, and risks—and, if all goes well, profits.

JP Morgan Private Bank adopted this model in 2007, at the onset of the global financial crisis. Risk managers, embedded within the line organization, report to both line executives and a centralized, independent risk-management function. The face-to-face contact with line managers enables the market-savvy risk managers to continually ask "what if" questions, challenging the assumptions of portfolio managers and forcing them to look at different scenarios. Risk managers assess how proposed trades affect the risk of the entire investment portfolio, not only under normal circumstances but also under times of extreme stress, when the correlations of returns across different asset classes escalate. "Portfolio managers come to me with three trades, and the [risk] model may say that all three are adding to the same type of risk," explains Gregoriy Zhikarev, a risk manager at JP Morgan. "Nine times out of 10 a manager will say, 'No, that's not what I want to do.' Then we can sit down and redesign the trades."

The chief danger from embedding risk managers within the line organization is that they "go native," aligning themselves with the inner circle of the business unit's leadership team—becoming deal makers rather than deal questioners. Preventing this is the responsibility of the company's senior risk officer and—ultimately—the CEO, who sets the tone for a company's risk culture.

Avoiding the Function Trap

Even if managers have a system that promotes rich discussions about risk, a second cognitive-behavioral trap awaits them. Because many strategy risks (and some external risks) are quite predictable—even familiar—companies tend to label and compartmentalize them, especially along business function lines. Banks often manage what they label "credit risk," "market risk," and "operational risk" in separate groups. Other companies compartmentalize the management of "brand risk," "reputation risk," "supply chain risk," "human resources risk," "IT risk," and "financial risk."

Such organizational silos disperse both information and responsibility for effective risk management. They inhibit discussion of how different risks interact. Good risk discussions must be not only confrontational but also integrative. Businesses can be derailed by a combination of small events that reinforce one another in unanticipated ways.

Managers can develop a companywide risk perspective by anchoring their discussions in strategic planning, the one integrative process that most well-run companies already have. For example, Infosys, the Indian IT services company, generates risk discussions from the Balanced Scorecard, its management tool for strategy measurement and communication. "As we asked ourselves about what risks we should be looking at," says M. D. Ranganath, the chief risk officer, "we gradually zeroed in on risks to business objectives specified in our corporate scorecard."

In building its Balanced Scorecard, Infosys had identified "growing client relationships" as a key objective and selected metrics for measuring progress, such as the number of global clients with annual billings in excess of $50 million and the annual percentage increases in revenues from large clients. In looking at the goal and the performance metrics together, management realized that its strategy had introduced a new risk factor: client default. When Infosys's business was based on numerous small clients, a single client default would not jeopardize the company's strategy. But a default by a $50 million client would present a major setback. Infosys began to monitor the credit default swap rate of every large client as a leading indicator of the likelihood of default. When a client's rate increased, Infosys would accelerate collection of receivables or request progress payments to reduce the likelihood or impact of default.

To take another example, consider Volkswagen do Brasil (subsequently abbreviated as VW), the Brazilian subsidiary of the

German carmaker. VW's risk-management unit uses the company's strategy map as a starting point for its dialogues about risk. For each objective on the map, the group identifies the risk events that could cause VW to fall short of that objective. The team then generates a Risk Event Card for each risk on the map, listing the practical effects of the event on operations, the probability of occurrence, leading indicators, and potential actions for mitigation. It also identifies who has primary accountability for managing the risk. (See the exhibit "The Risk Event Card.") The risk team then presents a high-level summary of results to senior management. (See the exhibit "The Risk Report Card.")

Beyond introducing a systematic process for identifying and mitigating strategy risks, companies also need a risk oversight structure. Infosys uses a dual structure: a central risk team that identifies general strategy risks and establishes central policy, and specialized functional teams that design and monitor policies and controls in consultation with local business teams. The decentralized teams have the authority and expertise to help the business lines respond to threats and changes in their risk profiles, escalating only the exceptions to the central risk team for review. For example, if a client relationship manager wants to give a longer credit period to a company whose credit risk parameters are high, the functional risk manager can send the case to the central team for review.

These examples show that the size and scope of the risk function are not dictated by the size of the organization. Hydro One, a large company, has a relatively small risk group to generate risk awareness and communication throughout the firm and to advise the executive team on risk-based resource allocations. By contrast, relatively small companies or units, such as JPL or JP Morgan Private Bank, need multiple project-level review boards or teams of embedded risk managers to apply domain expertise to assess the risk of business decisions. And Infosys, a large company with broad operational and strategic scope, requires a strong centralized risk-management function as well as dispersed risk managers who support local business decisions and facilitate the exchange of information with the centralized risk group.

The Risk Event Card

VW do Brasil uses Risk Event Cards to assess its strategy risks. First, managers document the risks associated with achieving each of the company's strategic objectives. For each identified risk, managers create a risk card that lists the practical effects of the event's occurring on operations. Below is a sample card looking at the effects of an interruption in deliveries, which could jeopardize VW's strategic objective of achieving a smoothly functioning supply chain.

Strategic objective	Risk event	Outcomes	Risk indicators	Likelihood/ consequences	Management controls	Accountable manager
Guarantee reliable and competitive supplier-to-manufacturer processes	Interruption of deliveries	Overtime	Critical items report		Hold daily supply chain meetings with logistics, purchasing, and QA	Mr. O. Manuel, director of manufacturing logistics
		Emergency freight	Late deliveries			
		Quality problems	Incoming defects		Monitor suppliers' tooling to detect deterioration	
		Production losses	Incorrect component shipments		Risk mitigation initiative: Upgrade suppliers' tooling	
					Risk mitigation initiative: Identify the key supply chain executive at each critical supplier	

The Risk Report Card

VW do Brasil summarizes its strategy risks on a Risk Report Card organized by strategic objectives (excerpt below). Managers can see at a glance how many of the identified risks for each objective are critical and require attention or mitigation. For instance, VW identified 11 risks associated with achieving the goal "Satisfy the customer's expectations." Four of the risks were critical, but that was an improvement over the previous quarter's assessment. Managers can also monitor progress on risk management across the company.

Strategic objective	Assessed risks	Critical risks	Trend
Achieve market share growth	4	1	↔
Satisfy the customer's expectations	11	4	↑
Improve company image	13	1	↔
Develop dealer organization	4	2	↔
Guarantee customer-oriented innovations management	5	2	↓
Achieve launch management efficiency	1	0	↔
Increase direct processes efficiency	4	1	↔
Create and manage a robust production volume strategy	2	1	↓
Guarantee reliable and competitive supplier-to-manufacturer processes	9	3	↔
Develop an attractive and innovative product portfolio	4	2	↓

Managing the Uncontrollable

External risks, the third category of risk, cannot typically be reduced or avoided through the approaches used for managing preventable and strategy risks. External risks lie largely outside the company's control; companies should focus on identifying them, assessing their potential impact, and figuring out how best to mitigate their effects should they occur.

Some external risk events are sufficiently imminent that managers can manage them as they do their strategy risks. For example, during the economic slowdown after the global financial crisis, Infosys identified a new risk related to its objective of developing a global workforce: an upsurge in protectionism, which could lead to tight restrictions on work visas and permits for foreign nationals in several OECD countries where Infosys had large client engagements. Although protectionist legislation is technically an external risk since it's beyond the company's control, Infosys treated it as a strategy risk and created a Risk Event Card for it, which included a new risk indicator: the number and percentage of its employees with dual citizenships or existing work permits outside India. If this number were to fall owing to staff turnover, Infosys's global strategy might be jeopardized. Infosys therefore put in place recruiting and retention policies that mitigate the consequences of this external risk event.

Most external risk events, however, require a different analytic approach either because their probability of occurrence is very low or because managers find it difficult to envision them during their normal strategy processes. We have identified several different sources of external risks:

- *Natural and economic disasters with immediate impact.* These risks are predictable in a general way, although their timing is usually not (a large earthquake will hit someday in California, but there is no telling exactly where or when). They may be anticipated only by relatively weak signals. Examples include natural disasters such as the 2010 Icelandic volcano eruption that closed European airspace for a week and economic disasters such as the bursting of a major asset price bubble. When these risks occur, their effects are typically drastic and immediate, as we saw in the disruption from the Japanese earthquake and tsunami in 2011.

- *Geopolitical and environmental changes with long-term impact.* These include political shifts such as major policy changes, coups, revolutions, and wars; long-term environmental changes such as global warming; and depletion of critical natural resources such as fresh water.

- *Competitive risks with medium-term impact.* These include the emergence of disruptive technologies (such as the internet, smartphones, and bar codes) and radical strategic moves by industry players (such as the entry of Amazon into book retailing and Apple into the mobile phone and consumer electronics industries).

Companies use different analytic approaches for each of the sources of external risk.

Tail-risk stress tests

Stress-testing helps companies assess major changes in one or two specific variables whose effects would be major and immediate, although the exact timing is not forecastable. Financial services firms use stress tests to assess, for example, how an event such as the tripling of oil prices, a large swing in exchange or interest rates, or the default of a major institution or sovereign country would affect trading positions and investments.

The benefits from stress-testing, however, depend critically on the assumptions—which may themselves be biased—about how much the variable in question will change. The tail-risk stress tests of many banks in 2007–2008, for example, assumed a worst-case scenario in which U.S. housing prices leveled off and remained flat for several periods. Very few companies thought to test what would happen if prices began to decline—an excellent example of the tendency to anchor estimates in recent and readily available data. Most companies extrapolated from recent U.S. housing prices, which had gone several decades without a general decline, to develop overly optimistic market assessments.

Scenario planning

This tool is suited for long-range analysis, typically five to 10 years out. Originally developed at Shell Oil in the 1960s, scenario analysis is a systematic process for defining the plausible boundaries of future states of the world. Participants examine political, economic, technological, social, regulatory, and environmental forces and select some number of drivers—typically four—that would have the biggest impact on the company. Some companies explicitly draw on the expertise in their advisory boards to inform them about significant trends, outside the company's and industry's day-to-day focus, that should be considered in their scenarios.

For each of the selected drivers, participants estimate maximum and minimum anticipated values over five to 10 years. Combining the extreme values for each of four drivers leads to 16 scenarios. About half tend to be implausible and are discarded; participants then assess how their firm's strategy would perform in the remaining scenarios. If managers see that their strategy is contingent on a generally optimistic view, they can modify it to accommodate pessimistic scenarios or develop plans for how they would change their strategy should early indicators show an increasing likelihood of events turning against it.

War-gaming

War-gaming assesses a firm's vulnerability to disruptive technologies or changes in competitors' strategies. In a war-game, the company assigns three or four teams the task of devising plausible near-term strategies or actions that existing or potential competitors might adopt during the next one or two years—a shorter time horizon than that of scenario analysis. The teams then meet to examine how clever competitors could attack the company's strategy. The process helps to overcome the bias of leaders to ignore evidence that runs counter to their current beliefs, including the possibility of actions that competitors might take to disrupt their strategy.

Companies have no influence over the likelihood of risk events identified through methods such as tail-risk testing, scenario planning, and war-gaming. But managers can take specific actions to mitigate their impact. Since moral hazard does not arise for non-preventable events, companies can use insurance or hedging to mitigate some risks, as an airline does when it protects itself against sharp increases in fuel prices by using financial derivatives. Another option is for firms to make investments now to avoid much higher costs later. For instance, a manufacturer with facilities in earthquake-prone areas can increase its construction costs to protect critical facilities against severe quakes. Also, companies exposed to different but comparable risks can cooperate to mitigate them. For example, the IT data centers of a university in North Carolina would be vulnerable to hurricane risk while those of a comparable university on the San Andreas Fault in California would be vulnerable to earthquakes. The likelihood that both disasters would happen on the same day is small enough that the two universities might choose to mitigate their risks by backing up each other's systems every night.

The Leadership Challenge

Managing risk is very different from managing strategy. Risk management focuses on the negative—threats and failures rather than opportunities and successes. It runs exactly counter to the "can do" culture most leadership teams try to foster when implementing strategy. And many leaders have a tendency to discount the future; they're reluctant to spend time and money now to avoid an uncertain future problem that might occur down the road, on someone else's watch. Moreover, mitigating risk typically involves dispersing resources and diversifying investments, just the opposite of the intense focus of a successful strategy. Managers may find it antithetical to their culture to champion processes that identify the risks to the strategies they helped formulate.

For those reasons, most companies need a separate function to handle strategy- and external-risk management. The risk function's size will vary from company to company, but the group must report directly to the top team. Indeed, nurturing a close relationship with senior leadership will arguably be its most critical task; a company's ability to weather storms depends very much on how seriously executives take their risk-management function when the sun is shining and no clouds are on the horizon.

That was what separated the banks that failed in the financial crisis from those that survived. The failed companies had relegated risk management to a compliance function; their risk managers had limited access to senior management and their boards of directors. Further, executives routinely ignored risk managers' warnings about highly leveraged and concentrated positions. By contrast, Goldman Sachs and JPMorgan Chase, two firms that weathered the financial crisis well, had strong internal risk-management functions and leadership teams that understood and managed the companies' multiple risk exposures. Barry Zubrow, chief risk officer at JP Morgan Chase, told us, "I may have the title, but [CEO] Jamie Dimon is the chief risk officer of the company."

Risk management is nonintuitive; it runs counter to many individual and organizational biases. Rules and compliance can mitigate some critical risks but not all of them. Active and cost-effective risk management requires managers to think systematically about the multiple categories of risks they face so that they can institute appropriate processes for each. These processes will neutralize their managerial bias of seeing the world as they would like it to be rather than as it actually is or could possibly become.

Originally published in June 2012. Reprint R1206B

How to Build Risk into Your Business Model

by Karan Girotra and Serguei Netessine

IN EARLY 2008 four entrepreneurs in Paris started MyFab, an internet-based furniture retailer that is doing more to change the industry than any other company since IKEA. Instead of building large stocks of furniture, as its competitors do, MyFab provides a catalog of potential designs. Customers vote on them, and the most popular ones are put into production and shipped to buyers directly from the manufacturing sites—with no retail outlets, inventories, complicated distribution, or logistics networks.

The engagement and social aspects of the voting attracted customers in droves, but they most loved the prices. By simplifying its supply chain and producing only what customers wanted, MyFab was able to offer products at significantly lower cost than established furniture retailers could. In just two years the company has grown to more than 100 employees; it now sells furniture and other products in four markets, including the United States.

MyFab did not identify new market segments, nor did it develop new products based on novel technology. In fact, its products are similar—often nearly identical—to those of its competitors. Like Dell, Zara, and Zipcar before it, MyFab has prospered by innovating its business model—the way it offers existing products or services that address existing customer needs using existing technologies. Very often this kind of innovation turns out to be more valuable and transformative than product- or technology-driven innovation, as readers of the work of Clay Christensen or INSEAD's W. Chan Kim and Renée Mauborgne well know.

But there's a perennial problem with business model innovation: Managers often find it harder to determine what changes to the model will work than whether a new product or technology will catch on. So what's the secret? How can companies systematically innovate their business models? How can executives identify and quantify the value of their changes? We believe that the literature on business model innovation has overlooked a critical driver of value: where in the value chain the risks associated with creating, supplying, and consuming products and services reside. In designing their value chains, companies typically focus on three things: revenue (price, market size, and ancillary sales), cost structure (direct and indirect costs, economies of scale and scope), and resource velocity (the rate at which value is created from the applied resources, typically captured through lead times, throughput, inventory turns, and asset utilization). These factors are well understood, and improving them is the main focus of management literature. Less well understood is that these value drivers are themselves affected by sharp changes in, for example, demand and supply. In thinking through changes to the business model, therefore, it is essential to examine the major sources of risk to the model and how the model will handle them.

Thinking in these terms quickly demonstrates the potential for companies to create value by redesigning their business models to reduce their risks. It can also reveal unsuspected opportunities for creating value by adding risk—if the company is well-placed to manage it. In the following pages we draw on our experience studying and consulting to dozens of companies—startups and large corporations alike—to describe the various types of risk-driven business model innovations and discuss their advantages and disadvantages.

Reducing Risks

Often companies that have lowered their business model risk have done so by delaying production commitments, transferring risk to other parties, or improving the quality of their information.

Idea in Brief

Many managers find it harder to tell if changes in their business models will work out than to guess whether a new product or technology will catch on.

The secret to systematic business model innovation is to focus on identifying where the risks are in your value chain. Then determine whether you can reduce them, shift them to other people, or even assume them yourself.

If you take this approach, you won't need extensive experimentation and prototyping to identify very powerful innovations, because many tools for managing risk are available.

Delaying production commitments

Speeding up the production process is the most obvious way to do this. It usually means producing in higher-cost locations, which goes against supply chain orthodoxy. But surprisingly often the gains from reducing demand uncertainty outweigh the added costs. This approach lies behind some very remarkable innovations.

Consider the famous Spanish clothing retailer Zara. Branded clothing companies have traditionally focused on managing costs by organizing their sourcing, production, and distribution as efficiently as possible. As a result, they may need as long as 12 to 18 months to design, produce, and deliver a new line of clothing. That means they have to make big bets on future consumer preferences and demand. Bearing this risk has consequences for the bottom line through inventory write-downs (if the clothes don't sell) or for the top line through stock-outs (if people want more than you've made).

Zara reduced the likelihood of these consequences by designing a hyperfast supply chain that turns a new line around in two to four weeks—making it much easier to keep pace with consumer preferences. Of course, there is a price: The company makes most of its products in an expensive location (southern Europe), ships them to stores often (weekly), and uses an expensive mode of transportation (air). But Zara's success demonstrates clearly that a focus on managing demand risks can trump a focus on costs.

Note that Zara did not discover anything new about the risks involved in retailing apparel. Everyone knows that customers are fickle and hard to read. Zara's insight was simply that a faster cycle time meant that decisions about product specifications and quantities needn't be made so far in advance, and fresher data would be available when the company did have to make commitments.

Reducing cycle time allows some companies to completely eliminate risks arising from demand uncertainty. Dell, for example, does not have to assemble a computer until the customer has ordered it, because it can turn the order around extremely fast. Again, a price must be paid: Like Zara, Dell must set up most of its production facilities close to its end customers (in the United States) and therefore cannot produce in low-cost locations for its main market. Similarly, Timbuk2, a popular bag manufacturer, can ship custom-designed orders to its customers in just two or three days—but its manufacturing has to be done in San Francisco rather than in China.

Rewriting your contracts

Another way to manage risk—especially asset-related risk—is to pass the exposure on to someone else. This usually involves altering your contracts with the other stakeholders in your value chain: employees, suppliers, and customers.

The customer-contact services provider LiveOps demonstrates how changing the terms of employment can radically alter a company's risk profile. Traditional providers of contact services maintain a workforce of customer service agents at a call center. The volume of service requests is highly variable, meaning that sometimes this workforce is underutilized for a large portion of the workday, but at other times the call volume far exceeds its capacity and customers must tolerate long waits. The usual solution is to relocate the contact center to a low-cost location such as India.

LiveOps turned this model on its head. Instead of employing and training a large workforce, it maintains a pool of loosely affiliated freelancers. These are often stay-at-home parents who cannot take a job with fixed hours but are available many times during the day.

The LiveOps computerized system allows them to work remotely in their free time. Agents log on to the system when they're available, and customer calls are routed to them. Most important, LiveOps pays the agents only for the time that they are on support calls—meaning that the employees themselves bear the risk of their underutilization. They are willing to assume this risk in return for being able to make their own hours and work from home.

In the late 1990s Blockbuster handed off risk to suppliers: It revolutionized the highly competitive video rental industry by shifting away from fixed-price contracts (under which each VHS tape cost Blockbuster $60) and toward revenue sharing with the major movie studios. Under the old arrangement, the studios took little risk in terms of a mismatch between demand and supply: They received $60 for a tape no matter how many times it was rented. Blockbuster assumed all the risk of acquiring a dud and had to hedge its bets by buying fewer tapes.

Under the new arrangement, Blockbuster paid only $5 to $10 up front but shared about 50% of its revenues with the studios. This changed the studios' information sharing, pricing, and marketing incentives, with the result that Blockbuster could stock more tapes, increasing the availability of hit movies. The company's market share rose from 25% to 38%, and profits for the industry grew by up to 20%.

Gathering better data

Sometimes it isn't possible to radically shorten the production process or alter your relationship with other stakeholders in your value chain. In that case, you can improve the quality of the information on which you base your commitments.

That is precisely what MyFab's customer voting system does. The actual process of making and delivering furniture quickly has been greatly refined, so relocating doesn't make as much competitive difference as it used to. The data MyFab gets through customer polling enable it to predict customer taste and demand levels more accurately than its competitors can, reducing its exposure to stock-outs and excess inventory.

The Next Big Thing?

THE IDEA OF AN ENVIRONMENTALLY FRIENDLY ELECTRIC CAR has been around for almost 100 years. Multiple product and technology innovations have steadily advanced this industry but so far have failed to create wide-scale adoption.

What are the risks for someone who decides to use an electric car?

The risk of running out of electricity in the middle of a trip. Current batteries last for only about 100 miles, and recharging them takes several hours.

The asset risk associated with owning a battery. The battery is very expensive, and technology evolves quickly, so the owner has to maximize battery use despite being unable to drive long distances.

Even when companies can reduce risk using the classic approaches, they should consider upgrading their information-gathering capabilities, because speeding up production or rewriting contracts often creates a new risk. This was a potential problem for LiveOps. Because its employees work from home and are independent contractors, it is much harder to verify that they are appropriately trained to answer calls. LiveOps mitigates this information risk by monitoring agents' performance and routing calls first to the higher-ranked agents.

Adding Risk

Many people regard risk only as something to eliminate—an undesirable concomitant of managing the resources and capabilities needed to deliver a product or service. But as the economist Robert Merton has often pointed out, one can also argue that companies create value by being better at managing risk than their competitors are. The implication is that if you are better than others at managing a particular risk, you should take on more of that risk.

The history of innovation demonstrates that quite a few companies have made money by taking on more risk—typically by changing

How could these risks be reduced for potential adopters?

Think about Zipcar. Take on risk by offering customers the ability to exchange depleted batteries for fully charged ones. This requires building battery-switching stations.

Look at Rolls-Royce. Double the risk by transferring battery ownership from the customer to the company and selling the customer "driving distance" one mile at a time. A company that owns thousands of batteries not only can ensure that the batteries are properly utilized but also will be better positioned to forecast technology evolution and amortize expensive assets.

These solutions may sound familiar: The Israeli startup Better Place has applied them both and is on track to enable electric-car adoption across Israel. Its business model innovation may achieve what technological and product innovation have long failed to deliver.

---

the terms of their contracts with suppliers or customers. More than 30 years ago Rolls-Royce, a manufacturer of aircraft engines, identified a major pain point in the industry: Maintaining airplane engines is rife with risk for the airlines. Engine breakdown can ground a plane for weeks while the airline pays for repair time and materials. Airlines, especially small ones, don't always have the resources to adequately provide for such breakdowns.

So, in the 1970s, Rolls-Royce started offering the airlines a very different service contract: "Power by the hour." The airlines would pay Rolls-Royce for an engine's flight hours rather than for repair time and materials. Of course, much of the risk reduction the airlines obtained was reflected in the price, but transferring the risk had a more profound effect: Rolls-Royce was motivated to improve its products and maintenance processes, because the fewer the problems and the quicker the fixes, the more the manufacturer got paid. The airlines could never have created value in this way, either on their own or by prodding Rolls-Royce, so the new contract triggered a completely new value creation dynamic. This movement, which is often referred to as servicization, has spilled over to other industries. For example, the German rail vehicle manufacturer Bombardier charges its customers for maintenance according to miles driven, and Caterpillar charges construction companies according to the amount of earth moved.

Sometimes trying to avoid a risk actually increases it, and you can better manage it by being willing to own more of it. Take the car rental business. The risk in this industry lies in underutilizing fixed assets—cars. Traditional companies rent in daily increments, so the customer has to pay for a day even if he needs the car for only a few hours. He must assume the risk of underutilized assets.

In 2000 Zipcar turned this model upside down. It realized that the ability to rent by the hour would encourage people to switch from taxis or limos to Zipcars. It could price its offering to improve on alternative short-distance transportation modes and still earn a much higher hourly rate than conventional car renters. (Zipcars cost about $8 an hour, whereas the prorated cost at a traditional company is $1 to $2.) The company's annual revenues are approaching $200 million, demonstrating that returns on its new model outweigh the costs of maintaining a large fleet and multiple pick-up and drop-off locations.

Advantages and Challenges

The risk-driven innovation we describe has one important advantage over other forms of innovation: It's much cheaper. Innovating products and technologies often involves generating a lot of ideas and then trimming the list down through discussion, voting, and prototyping. Multiple iterations of prototypes, customer feedback, and experimentation are necessary. Significant R&D expenditures are often involved.

Risk-driven innovation, however, can be approached in a systematic way and with few expenditures, and relatively clear and credible estimates can be made of the potential benefits and costs. A great deal of research has been done on the pricing of risk, and sound methods exist for putting a dollar value on contracts and real options that involve reducing, transferring, or adding risk. In fact, a recent article by Suzanne de Treville and Lenos Trigeorgis ("It May Be Cheaper to Manufacture at Home," HBR, October 2010) described how real options analysis lets you put a dollar value on the benefits of moving production from distant but cheap locations to close-by but expensive ones.

In addition, you don't need extensive experimentation and prototyping to identify very powerful innovations, because some of them have already been done and others can be quantified. Zipcar essentially reprised Rolls-Royce's approach, and Zara's innovation resembled Dell's. The sidebar "The Next Big Thing?" points out that a startup in Israel is borrowing ideas from Zipcar and Rolls-Royce to introduce an electric car on a large scale (see "How to Jump-Start the Clean-Tech Economy," by Mark W. Johnson and Josh Suskewicz, HBR, November 2009).

You might think that such innovations aren't a sustainable form of competitive advantage. But experience shows that they actually can be, because copying someone else's business model innovation often involves changing processes that are embedded in the culture of an organization—and substantially changing the cultural DNA is harder than adopting a new technology or design or entering a new market. It's particularly challenging when the company being copied is a competitor. Other car companies took decades to become as good as Ford is at mass production. And although the famous Toyota Production System is well described in numerous books, and anyone can visit a Toyota factory, U.S. automakers still struggle to implement it as effectively as Toyota does. Meanwhile, companies in other industries prospered mightily from being the first to adopt mass production or TPS.

The lesson: If you really want to steal a march on your rivals, shift some of the focus that you now put on improving your products and services to thinking about how you, your suppliers, and your customers can manage the risks of the business you conduct together.

Originally published in May 2011. Reprint R1105G

The Six Mistakes Executives Make in Risk Management

by Nassim N. Taleb, Daniel G. Goldstein, and Mark W. Spitznagel

WE DON'T LIVE in the world for which conventional risk-management textbooks prepare us. No forecasting model predicted the impact of the current economic crisis, and its consequences continue to take establishment economists and business academics by surprise. Moreover, as we all know, the crisis has been compounded by the banks' so-called risk-management models, which increased their exposure to risk instead of limiting it and rendered the global economic system more fragile than ever.

Low-probability, high-impact events that are almost impossible to forecast—we call them Black Swan events—are increasingly dominating the environment. Because of the internet and globalization, the world has become a complex system, made up of a tangled web of relationships and other interdependent factors. Complexity not only increases the incidence of Black Swan events but also makes forecasting even ordinary events impossible. All we can predict is that companies that ignore Black Swan events will go under.

Instead of trying to anticipate low-probability, high-impact events, we should reduce our vulnerability to them. Risk management, we believe, should be about lessening the impact of what we don't understand—not a futile attempt to develop sophisticated techniques and stories that perpetuate our illusions of being able to understand and predict the social and economic environment.

To change the way we think about risk, we must avoid making six mistakes.

1. We Think We Can Manage Risk by Predicting Extreme Events

This is the worst error we make, for a couple of reasons. One, we have an abysmal record of predicting Black Swan events. Two, by focusing our attention on a few extreme scenarios, we neglect other possibilities. In the process, we become more vulnerable.

It's more effective to focus on the consequences—that is, to evaluate the possible impact of extreme events. Realizing this, energy companies have finally shifted from predicting when accidents in nuclear plants might happen to preparing for the eventualities. In the same way, try to gauge how your company will be affected, compared with competitors, by dramatic changes in the environment. Will a small but unexpected fall in demand or supply affect your company a great deal? If so, it won't be able to withstand sharp drops in orders, sudden rises in inventory, and so on.

In our private lives, we sometimes act in ways that allow us to absorb the impact of Black Swan events. We don't try to calculate the odds that events will occur; we only worry about whether we can handle the consequences if they do. In addition, we readily buy insurance for health care, cars, houses, and so on. Does anyone buy a house and then check the cost of insuring it? You make your decision after taking into account the insurance costs. Yet in business we treat insurance as though it's an option. It isn't; companies must be prepared to tackle consequences and buy insurance to hedge their risks.

2. We Are Convinced That Studying the Past Will Help Us Manage Risk

Risk managers mistakenly use hindsight as foresight. Alas, our research shows that past events don't bear any relation to future shocks. World War I, the attacks of September 11, 2001—major

Idea in Brief

Conventional risk-management textbooks don't prepare us for the real world. For instance, no forecasting model predicted the impact of the 2008 economic crisis.

Managers make six common mistakes when confronting risk: They try to anticipate extreme events, they study the past for guidance, they disregard advice about what not to do, they use standard deviations to measure risk, they fail to recognize that mathematical equivalents can be psychologically different, and they believe there's no room for redundancy when it comes to efficiency.

Companies that ignore Black Swan (low-probability, high-impact) events will go under. But instead of trying to anticipate them, managers should reduce their companies' overall vulnerability.

events like those didn't have predecessors. The same is true of price changes. Until the late 1980s, the worst decline in stock prices in a single day had been around 10%. Yet prices tumbled by 23% on October 19, 1987. Why then would anyone have expected a meltdown after that to be only as little as 23%? History fools many.

You often hear risk managers—particularly those employed in the financial services industry—use the excuse "This is unprecedented." They assume that if they try hard enough, they can find precedents for anything and predict everything. But Black Swan events don't have precedents. In addition, today's world doesn't resemble the past; both interdependencies and nonlinearities have increased. Some policies have no effect for much of the time and then cause a large reaction.

People don't take into account the types of randomness inherent in many economic variables. There are two kinds, with socioeconomic randomness being less structured and tractable than the randomness you encounter in statistics textbooks and casinos. It causes winner-take-all effects that have severe consequences. Less than 0.25% of all the companies listed in the world represent around half the market capitalization, less than 0.2% of books account for approximately half their sales, less than 0.1% of drugs generate a little more than half the pharmaceutical industry's sales—and less than 0.1% of risky events will cause at least half your losses.

Because of socioeconomic randomness, there's no such thing as a "typical" failure or a "typical" success. There are typical heights and weights, but there's no such thing as a typical victory or catastrophe. We have to predict both an event and its magnitude, which is tough because impacts aren't typical in complex systems. For instance, when we studied the pharmaceuticals industry, we found that most sales forecasts don't correlate with new drug sales. Even when companies had predicted success, they underestimated drugs' sales by 22 times! Predicting major changes is almost impossible.

3. We Don't Listen to Advice about What We Shouldn't Do

Recommendations of the "don't" kind are usually more robust than "dos." For instance, telling someone not to smoke outweighs any other health-related advice you can provide. "The harmful effects of smoking are roughly equivalent to the combined good ones of every medical intervention developed since World War II. Getting rid of smoking provides more benefit than being able to cure people of every possible type of cancer," points out genetics researcher Druin Burch in *Taking the Medicine*. In the same vein, had banks in the U.S. heeded the advice not to accumulate large exposures to low-probability, high-impact events, they wouldn't be nearly insolvent today, although they would have made lower profits in the past.

Psychologists distinguish between acts of commission and those of omission. Although their impact is the same in economic terms—a dollar not lost is a dollar earned—risk managers don't treat them equally. They place a greater emphasis on earning profits than they do on avoiding losses. However, a company can be successful by preventing losses while its rivals go bust—and it can then take market share from them. In chess, grand masters focus on avoiding errors; rookies try to win. Similarly, risk managers don't like not to invest and thereby conserve value. But consider where you would be today if your investment portfolio had remained intact over the past two years, when everyone else's fell by 40%. Not losing almost half your retirement is undoubtedly a victory.

Positive advice is the province of the charlatan. The business sections in bookstores are full of success stories; there are far fewer tomes about failure. Such disparagement of negative advice makes companies treat risk management as distinct from profit making and as an afterthought. Instead, corporations should integrate risk-management activities into profit centers and treat them as profit-generating activities, particularly if the companies are susceptible to Black Swan events.

4. We Assume That Risk Can Be Measured by Standard Deviation

Standard deviation—used extensively in finance as a measure of investment risk—shouldn't be used in risk management. The standard deviation corresponds to the square root of average *squared* variations—not average variations. The use of squares and square roots makes the measure complicated. It only means that, in a world of tame randomness, around two-thirds of changes should fall within certain limits (the −1 and +1 standard deviations) and that variations in excess of seven standard deviations are practically impossible. However, this is inapplicable in real life, where movements can exceed 10, 20, or sometimes even 30 standard deviations. Risk managers should avoid using methods and measures connected to standard deviation, such as regression models, R-squares, and betas.

Standard deviation is poorly understood. Even quantitative analysts don't seem to get their heads around the concept. In experiments we conducted in 2007, we gave a group of quants information about the average absolute movement of a stock (the mean absolute deviation), and they promptly confused it with the standard deviation when asked to perform some computations. When experts are confused, it's unlikely that other people will get it right. In any case, anyone looking for a single number to represent risk is inviting disaster.

5. We Don't Appreciate That What's Mathematically Equivalent Isn't Psychologically So

In 1965, physicist Richard Feynman wrote in *The Character of Physical Law* that two mathematically equivalent formulations can be unequal in the sense that they present themselves to the human mind in different ways. Similarly, our research shows that the way a risk is framed influences people's understanding of it. If you tell investors that, on average, they will lose all their money only every 30 years, they are more likely to invest than if you tell them they have a 3.3% chance of losing a certain amount each year.

The same is true of airplane rides. We asked participants in an experiment: "You are on vacation in a foreign country and are considering flying the national airline to see a special island you have always wondered about. Safety statistics in this country show that if you flew this airline once a year there would be one crash every 1,000 years on average. If you don't take the trip, it is extremely unlikely you'll revisit this part of the world again. Would you take the flight?" All the respondents said they would.

We then changed the second sentence so it read: "Safety statistics show that, on average, one in 1,000 flights on this airline has crashed." Only 70% of the sample said they would take the flight. In both cases, the chance of a crash is 1 in 1,000; the latter formulation simply sounds more risky.

Providing a best-case scenario usually increases the appetite for risk. Always look for the different ways in which risk can be presented to ensure that you aren't being taken in by the framing or the math.

6. We Are Taught That Efficiency and Maximizing Shareholder Value Don't Tolerate Redundancy

Most executives don't realize that optimization makes companies vulnerable to changes in the environment. Biological systems cope with change; Mother Nature is the best risk manager of all. That's partly because she loves redundancy. Evolution has given us spare parts—we have two lungs and two kidneys, for instance—that allow us to survive.

In companies, redundancy consists of apparent inefficiency: idle capacities, unused parts, and money that isn't put to work. The opposite is leverage, which we are taught is good. It isn't; debt makes companies—and the economic system—fragile. If you are highly leveraged, you could go under if your company misses a sales forecast, interest rates change, or other risks crop up. If you aren't carrying debt on your books, you can cope better with changes.

Overspecialization hampers companies' evolution. David Ricardo's theory of comparative advantage recommended that for optimal efficiency, one country should specialize in making wine, another in manufacturing clothes, and so on. Arguments like this ignore unexpected changes. What will happen if the price of wine collapses? In the 1800s many cultures in Arizona and New Mexico vanished because they depended on a few crops that couldn't survive changes in the environment.

One of the myths about capitalism is that it is about incentives. It is also about disincentives. No one should have a piece of the upside without a share of the downside. However, the very nature of compensation adds to risk. If you give someone a bonus without clawback provisions, he or she will have an incentive to hide risk by engaging in transactions that have a high probability of generating small profits and a small probability of blowups. Executives can thus collect bonuses for several years. If blowups eventually take place, the managers may have to apologize but won't have to return past bonuses. This applies to corporations, too. That's why many CEOs become rich while shareholders stay poor. Society and shareholders should have the legal power to get back the bonuses of those who fail us. That would make the world a better place.

Moreover, we shouldn't offer bonuses to those who manage risky establishments such as nuclear plants and banks. The chances are that they will cut corners in order to maximize profits. Society gives its greatest risk-management task to the military, but soldiers don't get bonuses.

Remember that the biggest risk lies within us: We overestimate our abilities and underestimate what can go wrong. The ancients considered hubris the greatest defect, and the gods punished it mercilessly. Look at the number of heroes who faced fatal retribution for their hubris: Achilles and Agamemnon died as a price of their arrogance; Xerxes failed because of his conceit when he attacked Greece; and many generals throughout history have died for not recognizing their limits. Any corporation that doesn't recognize its Achilles' heel is fated to die because of it.

Originally published in October 2009. Reprint R0910G

From Superstorms to Factory Fires

Managing Unpredictable Supply-Chain Disruptions.

by David Simchi-Levi, William Schmidt, and Yehua Wei

TRADITIONAL METHODS FOR managing supply chain risk rely on knowing the likelihood of occurrence and the magnitude of impact for every potential event that could materially disrupt a firm's operations. For common supply-chain disruptions—poor supplier performance, forecast errors, transportation breakdowns, and so on—those methods work very well, using historical data to quantify the level of risk.

But it's a different story for low-probability, high-impact events—megadisasters like Hurricane Katrina in 2005, viral epidemics like the 2003 SARS outbreak, or major outages due to unforeseen events such as factory fires and political upheavals. Because historical data on these rare events are limited or nonexistent, their risk is hard to quantify using traditional models. As a result, many companies do not adequately prepare for them. That can have calamitous consequences when catastrophes do strike and can force even operationally savvy companies to scramble after the fact—think of Toyota following the 2011 Fukushima earthquake and tsunami.

To address this challenge, we developed a model—a mathematical description of the supply chain that can be computerized—that focuses on the impact of potential failures at points along the supply chain (such as the shuttering of a supplier's factory or a flood at a distribution center), rather than the cause of the disruption. This type of analysis obviates the need to determine the probability that any specific risk will occur—a valid approach since the mitigation strategies for a disruption are equally effective regardless of what caused it. Using the model, companies can quantify what the financial and operational impact would be if a critical supplier's facility were out of commission for, say, two weeks—whatever the reason. The computerized model can be updated easily and quickly, which is crucial since supply chains are in a continual state of flux.

In developing and applying our model at Ford Motor Company and other firms, we were surprised to find little correlation between how much a firm spends annually on procurement at a particular site and the impact that the site's disruption would have on company performance. Indeed, as the Ford case study described later in this article shows, the greatest exposures often lie in unlikely places.

In practice, that means that leaders using traditional risk-management techniques and simple heuristics (dollar amount spent at a site, for instance) often end up focusing exclusively on the so-called strategic suppliers for whom expenditures are very high and whose parts are deemed crucial to product differentiation, and overlooking the risks associated with low-cost, commodity suppliers. As a result, managers take the wrong actions, waste resources, and leave the organization exposed to hidden risk. In this article, we describe our model and how companies can use it to identify, manage, and reduce their exposure to supply chain risks.

Time to Recovery and the Risk Exposure Index

A central feature of our model is time to recovery (TTR): the time it would take for a particular node (such as a supplier facility, a distribution center, or a transportation hub) to be restored to full functionality after a disruption. TTR values are determined by examining historical experience and surveying the firm's buyers or suppliers (see the sidebar "Assessing Impact? Use a Simple Questionnaire"). These values can be unique for every node or can differ across a subset of the nodes.

Idea in Brief

The Problem

Traditional tools for analyzing supply chain risks require assessments of whether something is likely to happen, and the magnitude of its impact.

Why This Happens

A large class of risks—such as tsunamis, pandemics, and strikes—can't be assessed in this way.

The Solution

The authors have developed a model for determining the impact that a disruption of each node in its supply chain would have, regardless of its cause or likelihood. It uncovers risks that other models don't, including dangers posed by suppliers of low-cost commodities and the lack of correlation between the impact of a site disruption and dollar amount that the firm spends at that site.

Our model integrates TTR data with information on multiple tiers of supplier relationships, bill-of-material information, operational and financial measures, in-transit and on-site inventory levels, and demand forecasts for each product. Firms can represent their entire supply network at any level of detail—from individual parts to aggregations based on part category, supplier, geography, or product line. This allows managers to drill down into greater detail as needed and identify previously unrecognized dependencies. The model can account for disruptions of varying severity by running scenarios using TTRs of different durations.

To conduct the analysis, the model removes one node at a time from the supply network for the duration of the TTR. It then determines the supply chain response that would minimize the performance impact of the disruption at that node—for instance, drawing down inventory, shifting production, expediting transportation, or reallocating resources. On the basis of the optimal response, it generates a financial or operational performance impact (PI) for the node. A company can choose different measures of PI: lost units of production, revenue, or profit margin, for instance. The model analyzes all nodes in the network, assigning a PI to each. The node with the largest PI (in lost sales, for instance, or lost units of production)

Assessing Impact? Use a Simple Questionnaire

THE FIRST STEP IN ASSESSING THE RISK associated with a particular supplier is to calculate time to recovery (TTR) for each of its sites under various disruption scenarios. Companies can develop a simple survey to collect key data, including:

1. *Supplier*
   - Site location (city, region, country)

2. *Parts from this site*
   - Part number and description
   - Part cost
   - Annual volume for this part
   - Inventory information (days of supply) for this part
   - Total spend (per year) from this site

3. *End product*
   - OEM's end product(s) that uses this part
   - Profit margin for the end product(s)

4. *Lead times from supplier site to OEM sites*
   - Days

---

is assigned a risk exposure index (REI) score of 1.0. All other nodes' REI scores are indexed relative to this value (a node whose disruption would cause the least impact receives a value close to zero). The indexed scores allow the firm to identify at a glance the nodes that should get the most attention from risk managers.

At its core, the model uses a common mathematical technique—linear optimization—to determine the best response to a node's being disrupted for the duration of its TTR. The model accounts for existing and alternative sources of supply, transportation, inventory of finished goods, work in progress and raw material, and production dependencies within the supply chain.

5. *Time to recovery (TTR)*

The time it would take for the site to be restored to full functionality

- if the supplier site is down, but the tooling is not damaged

- if the tooling is lost

6. *Cost of loss*

- Is expediting components from other locations possible? If so, what is the cost?

- Can additional resources (overtime, more shifts, alternate capacity) be organized to satisfy demand? If so, what is the cost?

7. *Supplier risk assessment*

- Does the supplier produce only from a single source?

- Could alternate vendors supply the part?

- Is the supplier financially stable?

- Is there variability in performance (lead time, fill rate, quality)?

8. *Mitigation strategies for this supplier-part combination*

- Alternate suppliers

- Excess inventory

- Other

Our approach provides a number of benefits. It:

Identifies hidden exposures

The model helps managers identify which nodes in the network create the greatest risk exposure—often highlighting previously hidden or overlooked areas of high risk. It also allows the firm to compare the costs and benefits of various alternatives for mitigating impact.

Avoids the need for predictions about rare events

The model determines the optimal response to any disruption that might occur within the supply network, regardless of the cause.

Rather than trying to quantify the likelihood that a low-probability, high-risk event will strike, firms can focus on identifying the most important exposures and putting in place risk-management strategies to mitigate them.

Reveals supply chain dependencies and bottlenecks

Companies can also use the analyses to make inventory and sourcing decisions that increase the robustness of the network. This includes taking into account the likely scramble among rival companies to lock in alternative sources if a supplier's disruption affects several firms. Such cross-firm effects of a crisis are often overlooked. Contracts with backup suppliers can be negotiated to give a company priority over others should a disruption with the primary supplier occur, which would decrease time to recovery and financial impact.

Promotes discussion and learning

In the course of analyzing the supply chain in this way, managers engage in discussions with suppliers and internal groups about acceptable levels of TTR for critical facilities and share insights about best-practice processes to reduce recovery time. As a result, the impact of disruptions is minimized.

Prescriptive Actions

Our model provides organizations with a quantitative metric for segmenting suppliers by risk level. Using data generated by the model, we can categorize suppliers along two dimensions: the total amount of money that the company spends at each supplier site in a given year, and the performance impact on the firm associated with a disruption of each supplier node. Let's now take a look at the supplier segments and consider the risk-management strategies appropriate for each.

Obvious high risk

Most companies focus their risk-management activities on suppliers for whom total spend and performance impact are both high.

Typically, these are the suppliers of expensive components, such as car seats and instrument panels, that strongly affect customers' purchase decisions and experience. The cost of these "strategic components," as they're frequently called, often make up a large portion of the total manufacturing cost. Indeed, for many companies, they represent 20% of the suppliers but account for about 80% of a firm's total procurement expenditures. Because strategic components typically come from a single supplier, appropriate risk-mitigation strategies include strategic partnering with the suppliers to analyze and reduce their risk exposure, providing incentives to some suppliers to have multiple manufacturing sites in different regions, tracking suppliers' performance, and developing and implementing business continuity plans.

Low risk

Suppliers with low total spend and low financial impact do not require intense risk-management investment. In our experience, most companies effectively manage the minimal risks from disruptions of these supplier sites by investing in excess inventory or negotiating long-term contracts with a penalty clause for nonperformance.

Hidden risk

Many companies, however, are subject to considerable exposure from "hidden risk" suppliers. Here, total spend is low but the financial impact of a disruption is high. Even the savviest managers are prone to equating total spend with performance impact: They rightly identify strategic components as carrying high levels of supply chain risk, but fail to consider that low-spend suppliers, often of commodity goods, may represent outsize risks. Traditional risk-assessment exercises overlook these components because they are perceived as adding little value to the firm's products. But the reality is that markets for commodity goods are typically dominated by only a few manufacturers, leaving purchasers susceptible to disruptions. For example, in the automotive industry, a carmaker's total spend on suppliers of O-rings or valves is typically quite low, but if the supply is disrupted, the carmaker will have to shut down the production line. Thus, it is critical to ensure that an adequate supply is available. That can often be accomplished using the strategies that apply to the other segments: investing in excess inventory, requiring suppliers to operate multiple production sites, or implementing dual-sourcing strategies.

Alternatively, companies can use flexibility to deal with hidden supply risks. For example, system flexibility (the ability to quickly change the production mix of plants) allowed Pepsi Bottling Group to rapidly respond to a supply disruption caused by a fire at a chemical plant near one of its suppliers. Similarly, product-design flexibility (in this case, the use of standardized components) enabled Nokia to recover quickly from a disruption of its supply of radio frequency chips caused by a fire at a supplier's factory. Finally, process flexibility (achieved in this case by adjusting workforce skills and processes) allowed Toyota to quickly restore the supply of brake-fluid-proportioning valves (P-valves) after a major disruption.

Case Study: Ford Motor Company

We used our methodology to analyze Ford's exposure to supply chain disruptions. Working together with Keith W. Combs, Steve J. Faraci, Oleg Y. Gusikhin, and Don X. Zhang, managers in Ford's purchasing and R&D groups, we looked at two scenarios: In the first, the supplier's production facility is disrupted for two weeks. In the second,

---

A high-tech manufacturer's risk exposure index

Our model allows companies in any industry to effectively identify areas of hidden risk in the supply chain. Imagine a high-tech manufacturer that has suppliers and assembly plants all over the world. For each node in the supply chain, managers estimate the time to recovery if a disruption occurred at that node (how long it would take for the node to be restored to full operation) and then calculate the performance impact (lost sales during TTR, for instance). By indexing the performance impact values, managers can see at a glance which nodes represent the highest risks and direct their mitigation strategies accordingly.

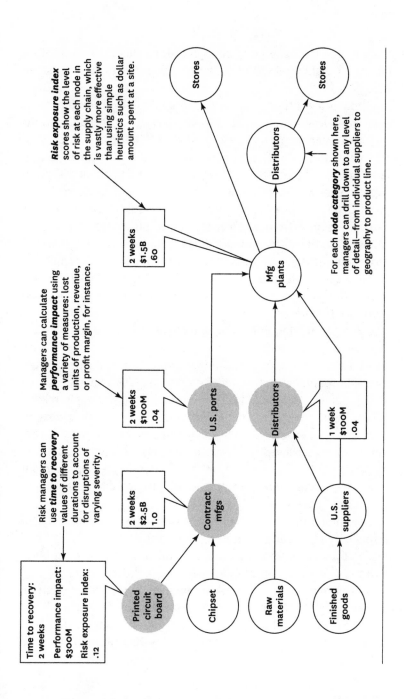

Risk exposure index scores show the level of risk at each node in the supply chain, which is vastly more effective than using simple heuristics such as dollar amount spent at a site.

Managers can calculate **performance impact** using a variety of measures: lost units of production, revenue, or profit margin, for instance.

Risk managers can use **time to recovery** values of different durations to account for disruptions of varying severity.

Time to recovery: 2 weeks

Performance impact: $300M

Risk exposure index: .12

For each **node category** shown here, managers can drill down to any level of detail—from individual suppliers to geography to product line.

Stores

Stores

Distributors

2 weeks
$1.5B
.60

Mfg plants

Distributors

2 weeks
$100M
.04

U.S. ports

Distributors

1 week
$100M
.04

2 weeks
$2.5B
1.0

Contract mfgs

Printed circuit board

Chipset

Raw materials

Finished goods

U.S. suppliers

the supplier's tooling must be replaced, halting operations at its facility for eight weeks. (Details have been altered to mask sensitive Ford data.)

Ford has a multitier supplier network with long lead times from some suppliers, a complex bill-of-materials structure, buffer inventory, and components that are shared across multiple product lines. Approximately 61% of the supplier sites would have no impact on Ford's profits if they were disrupted. By contrast, about 2% of the supplier sites would, if disrupted, have a significant impact on Ford's profits. The supplier sites whose disruption would cause the greatest damage are those from which Ford's annual purchases are relatively small—a finding that surprised Ford managers. Indeed, many of those suppliers had not previously been identified by the company's risk managers as high-exposure suppliers. (See the exhibit "Impact of supplier disruptions on Ford's profits" for an analysis of 1,000 Ford supplier sites.)

Using the model, Ford was able to identify the supplier sites that required no special risk-management attention (those with short TTR and low financial impact) and those that warranted more-thorough disruption-mitigation plans. The results from the analysis allowed Ford to evaluate alternative steps it might take to defuse high-impact risks and to better prioritize its risk mitigation strategies. For example, managers learned that the risk-exposure-index scores associated with certain suppliers are highly sensitive to the amount of inventory the firm carries. For that reason, Ford put processes in place to monitor the inventory related to those suppliers on a daily basis.

In March 2012, the auto industry was rocked by a shortage of a specialty resin called nylon 12, used in the manufacture of fuel tanks, brake components, and seat fabrics. The key supplier, Evonik, had experienced a devastating explosion in its plant in Marl, Germany. It took Evonik six months to restart production, during which time the downstream production facilities of Ford and other major automakers were severely disrupted. Had Ford managers used our framework prior to this disruption, they would have detected the risk exposure and associated production bottle-neck and proactively worked with Evonik to fast-track its plans to bring online a new plant in Singapore, currently slated to begin production in 2015.

Ford's supply chain, like those of many other companies, has become increasingly globalized, complex, and extended. This has had the effect of introducing more potential points of failure that Ford must recognize and manage. Using our model, it can rapidly quantify its supply chain exposure and identify effective strategies to mitigate the impact should disruptions occur.

Impact of supplier disruptions on Ford's profits

The sites whose disruption would cause the greatest damage are those from which Ford's annual purchases are relatively small. Ford had not previously identified many of them as high-exposure suppliers. (Data have been disguised to protect sensitive competitive information.)

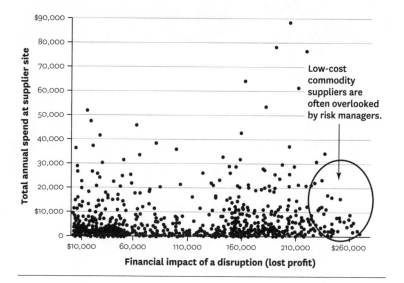

Our approach to managing supply chain risks allows managers to avoid guessing the likelihood of infrequent, high-impact events and instead concentrate on evaluating their organization's vulnerability to disruptions, regardless of their cause and where they strike. The method is quantitative, produces a risk exposure measure that is easy to understand, and supports a supplier segmentation process that results in supply networks that are much more resilient.

Originally published in January–February 2014. Reprint R1401H

Is It Real? Can We Win? Is It Worth Doing?

Managing Risk and Reward in an Innovation Portfolio.
by George S. Day

MINOR INNOVATIONS MAKE up 85% to 90% of companies' development portfolios, on average, but they rarely generate the growth companies seek. At a time when companies should be taking bigger—but smart—innovation risks, their bias is in the other direction. From 1990 to 2004 the percentage of major innovations in development portfolios dropped from 20.4 to 11.5—even as the number of growth initiatives rose.[1] The result is internal traffic jams of safe, incremental innovations that delay all projects, stress organizations, and fail to achieve revenue goals.

These small projects, which I call "little i" innovations, are necessary for continuous improvement, but they don't give companies a competitive edge or contribute much to profitability. It's the risky "Big I" projects—new to the company or new to the world—that push the firm into adjacent markets or novel technologies and can generate the profits needed to close the gap between revenue forecasts and growth goals. (According to one study, only 14% of new-product launches were substantial innovations, but they accounted for 61% of all profit from innovations among the companies examined.[2])

The aversion to Big I projects stems from a belief that they are too risky and their rewards (if any) will accrue too far in the future. Certainly the probability of failure rises sharply when a company ventures beyond incremental initiatives within familiar markets. But avoiding risky projects altogether can strangle growth. The solution is to pursue a disciplined, systematic process that will distribute your innovations more evenly across the spectrum of risk.

Two tools, used in tandem, can help companies do this. The first, the risk matrix, will graphically reveal risk exposure across an entire innovation portfolio. The second, the R-W-W ("real, win, worth it") screen, originated by Dominick ("Don") M. Schrello, of Long Beach, California, can be used to evaluate individual projects. Versions of the screen have been circulating since the 1980s, and since then a growing roster of companies, including General Electric, Honeywell, Novartis, Millipore, and 3M, have used them to assess business potential and risk exposure in their innovation portfolios; 3M has used R-W-W for more than 1,500 projects. I have expanded the screen and used it to evaluate dozens of projects at four global companies, and I have taught executives and Wharton students how to use it as well.

Although both tools, and the steps within them, are presented sequentially here, their actual use is not always linear. The information derived from each one can often be reapplied in later stages of development, and the two tools may inform each other. Usually, development teams quickly discover when and how to improvise on the tools' structured approach in order to maximize learning and value.

The Risk Matrix

To balance its innovation portfolio, a company needs a clear picture of how its projects fall on the spectrum of risk. The risk matrix employs a unique scoring system and calibration of risk to help estimate the probability of success or failure for each project based on how big a stretch it is for the firm: The less familiar the intended market (x axis) and the product or technology (y axis), the higher the risk. (See the exhibit "Assessing risk across an innovation portfolio.")

Idea in Brief

Incremental innovations (small, safe changes to your firm's offerings) make up 85%-90% of companies' development portfolios. But "little i" projects rarely produce competitive advantage. For that, you need "Big I" innovations—offerings new to your organization or the world. Yes, they're risky. But avoid them, and you may strangle your company's growth.

Day recommends a solution: increase the proportion of major innovations in your portfolio while carefully managing their risks. Two tools can help:

- A **risk matrix** enables you to estimate each project's probability of success or failure based on how big a stretch it is for your firm. The less familiar the intended market and the product or technology, the higher the risk.

- The **R-W-W ("real," "win," "worth it") screen** helps you evaluate projects' feasibility. The first step in using this tool— asking "is it real" questions— helps you determine whether customers want your innovation and, if so, whether you can build it.

A project's position on the matrix is determined by its score on a range of factors, such as how closely the behavior of targeted customers will match that of the company's current customers, how relevant the company's brand is to the intended market, and how applicable its technology capabilities are to the new product.

A portfolio review team—typically consisting of senior managers with strategic oversight and authority over development budgets and allocations—conducts the evaluation, with the support of each project's development team. Team members rate each project independently and then explain their rationale. They discuss reasons for any differences of opinion and seek consensus. The resulting scores serve as a project's coordinates on the risk matrix.

The determination of each score requires deep insights. When McDonald's attempted to offer pizza, for example, it assumed that the new offering was closely adjacent to its existing ones, and thus targeted its usual customers. Under that assumption, pizza would be a familiar product for the present market and would appear in the bottom left of the risk matrix. But the project failed, and a

Idea in Practice

Using the Risk Matrix

Assemble a team to assess each innovation project's potential risk using these criteria:

- How closely target customers' behavior will match current customers'

- How relevant the company's brand is to the intended market

- How applicable your capabilities are to the new product

Neglect to assess risk, and you may make a major misstep.

Example: When McDonald's started offering pizza, it assumed the new product was closely adjacent to existing ones. So it targeted its usual customers. But employees couldn't make and serve a pizza within 30 seconds—which violated McDonald's service-delivery model. And the company's brand didn't give "permission" to offer pizza. The project failed.

Using the R-W-W screen

Used throughout a product's development, the R-W-W screen exposes faulty assumptions, knowledge gaps, sources of risk, and problems suggesting termination. To employ this tool, repeatedly test each project's viability according to these criteria:

Is it real?

A **market** exists for the product if:	The **product** is real if:
<ul><li>There's a need or desire for the product.</li><li>Customers can buy it (for example, they have the money).</li><li>There are enough potential buyers.</li><li>Consumers will buy (for instance, they're willing to switch to your offering).</li></ul>	<ul><li>It has precisely described characteristics.</li><li>It can be produced with available technology and materials.</li><li>It will satisfy the market in its final form.</li></ul>

Can we win?

The **product** will be competitive if:	Your **company** will be competitive if:
• It offers clear advantages over alternatives, such as greater safety or social acceptability (think hybrid cars). • Those advantages can be sustained (for example, through patents). • It can survive competitors' responses (such as a price war).	• It has superior resources (such as engineering or logistics). • Managers have experience in the market and skills appropriate for the project's scale and complexity. • Projects have champions who can energize development teams, sell the vision to senior management, and overcome adversity. • It has mastery of market research tools and shares customers' insights with development-team members.

Is it worth doing?

The product will be **profitable** at an acceptable risk if:	The product makes **strategic sense** if:
• Its forecasted returns are greater than costs—considering matters such as the timing and amount of capital outlays, marketing expenses, breakeven time, and the cost of product extensions needed to keep ahead of competitors.	• It fits with your company's growth strategy; for example, by enhancing customer relationships or creating opportunities for follow-on business.

Assessing risk across an innovation portfolio

The risk matrix*

This tool will reveal the distribution of risk across a company's innovation portfolio. Each innovation can be positioned on the matrix by determining its score on two dimensions—how familiar to the company the intended market is (x axis) and how familiar the product or technology is (y axis)—using the grid "Positioning projects on the matrix." Familiar products aimed at the company's current markets will fall in the bottom left of the matrix, indicating a low probability of failure. New products aimed at unfamiliar markets will fall in the upper right, revealing a high probability of failure.

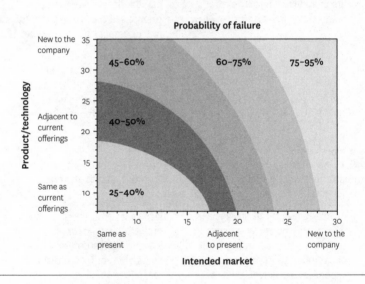

postmortem showed that the launch had been fraught with risk: Because no one could figure out how to make and serve a pizza in 30 seconds or less, orders caused long backups, violating the McDonald's service-delivery model. The postmortem also revealed that the company's brand didn't give "permission" to offer pizza. Even though its core fast-food customers were demographically similar to pizza lovers, their expectations about the McDonald's experience didn't include pizza.

Risk and revenue

Each dot on this risk matrix stands for one innovation in an imaginary company's portfolio. The size of each dot is proportional to the project's estimated revenue. (Companies may choose to illustrate estimated development investment or some other financial measure instead.) This portfolio, dominated by relatively low-risk, low-reward projects, is typical in its distribution.

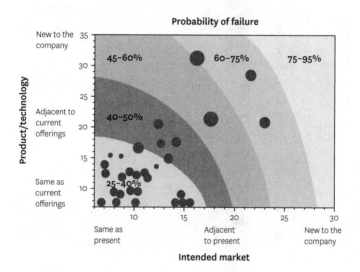

(continued)

Once the risk matrix has been completed, it typically reveals two things: that a company has more projects than it can manage well, and that the distribution of Big I and little i innovations is lopsided. Most companies will find that the majority of their projects cluster in the bottom left quadrant of the matrix, and a minority skew toward the upper right.

This imbalance is unhealthy if unsurprising. Discounted cash flow analysis and other financial yardsticks for evaluating development projects are usually biased against the delayed payoffs and uncertainty inherent in Big I innovations. What's more, little i projects tend to drain R&D budgets as companies struggle to keep up

Assessing risk across an innovation portfolio (continued)

Positioning projects on the matrix

Position each innovation product or concept by completing each statement in the left-hand column with one of the options offered across the top to arrive at a score from 1 to 5. Add the six scores in the "intended market" section to determine the project's x-axis coordinate. Add the seven scores in the "Product/technology" section to determine its y-axis coordinate.

	Intended market		
	...be the same as in our present market	...partially overlap with our present market	...be entirely different from our present market or are unknown
Customers' behavior and decision-making processes will...	1	2	3	4	5
Our distribution and sales activities will...	1	2	3	4	5
The competitive set (incumbents or potential entrants) will...	1	2	3	4	5
	...highly relevant	...somewhat relevant	...not at all relevant
Our brand promise is...	1	2	3	4	5
Our current customer relationships are...	1	2	3	4	5
Our knowledge of competitors' behavior and intentions is...	1	2	3	4	5
			Total (x-axis coordinate)

Product/technology

	...is fully applicable		...will require significant adaptation		...is not applicable
Our current development capability...	1	2	3	4	5
Our technology competency...	1	2	3	4	5
Our intellectual property protection...	1	2	3	4	5
Our manufacturing and service delivery system...	1	2	3	4	5

	...are identical to those of our current offerings		...overlap somewhat with those of our current offerings		...completely differ from those of our current offerings
The required knowledge and science bases...	1	2	3	4	5
The necessary product and service functions...	1	2	3	4	5
The expected quality standards...	1	2	3	4	5

Total
(y-axis coordinate)

*This risk matrix was developed from many sources, including long-buried consulting reports by A. T. Kearney and other firms, the extensive literature on the economic performance of acquisitions and alliances, and numerous audits of product and service innovations. It broadly defines "failure" as significantly missing the objectives that were used to justify the investment in the growth initiative. Estimates of the probability of failure have been thoroughly validated in dozens of interviews with consultants and senior managers involved in innovation initiatives and are consistent with recent surveys that place the overall failure rate of new products close to 40%. The ranges in probabilities take into account some of the variability in organizations' definitions of failure and in what constitutes a new market or technology for a given company. The probabilities do not apply to fast-moving consumer goods (where incremental innovations have high long-run failure rates) or ethical pharmaceuticals, and don't distinguish whether "new to the company" innovations are also new to the world. (Although these are distinct categories, in my experience most major new-to-the-company innovations are also new to the world; for the purposes of this article, they're considered to be broadly overlapping.) "Market" refers to customers, not geographies.

with customers' and salespeople's demands for a continuous flow of incrementally improved products. The risk matrix creates a visual starting point for an ongoing dialogue about the company's mix of projects and their fit with strategy and risk tolerance. The next step is to look closely at each project's prospects in the marketplace.

Screening with R-W-W

The R-W-W screen is a simple but powerful tool built on a series of questions about the innovation concept or product, its potential market, and the company's capabilities and competition (see the exhibit "Screening for success"). It is not an algorithm for making go/no-go decisions but, rather, a disciplined process that can be employed at multiple stages of product development to expose faulty assumptions, gaps in knowledge, and potential sources of risk, and to ensure that every avenue for improvement has been explored. The R-W-W screen can be used to identify and help fix problems that are miring a project, to contain risk, and to expose problems that can't be fixed and therefore should lead to termination.

Innovation is inherently messy, nonlinear, and iterative. For simplicity, this article focuses on using the R-W-W screen in the early stages to test the viability of product concepts. In reality, however, a given product would be screened repeatedly during development—at the concept stage, during prototyping, and early in the launch planning. Repeated assessment allows screeners to incorporate increasingly detailed product, market, and financial analyses into the evaluation, yielding ever more accurate answers to the screening questions.

R-W-W guides a development team to dig deeply for the answers to six fundamental questions: *Is the market real? Is the product real? Can the product be competitive? Can our company be competitive? Will the product be profitable at an acceptable risk? Does launching the product make strategic sense?*

The development team answers these queries by exploring an even deeper set of supporting questions. The team determines where the answer to each question falls on a continuum ranging

Screening for success

*Each product concept in your company's innovation portfolio should be
assessed by its development team using the R-W-W screen below. A definite
yes or no answer to the first-column questions Is it real?, Can we win?, and Is
it worth doing? requires digging deeply for robust answers to the supporting
questions in the second and third columns. Often a team will answer maybe;
its goal should be to investigate all possible avenues to converting no or
maybe into yes. A definite no to any second-column question typically leads to
termination of the project, since failure is all but certain. A definite no to any
third-column question argues strongly against proceeding with development.
(The full set of questions in columns two and three of the screen come from
evaluations of more than 50 product failures within two companies I worked
with by teams of auditors who asked, "What questions, properly answered,
might have prevented the failure?")*

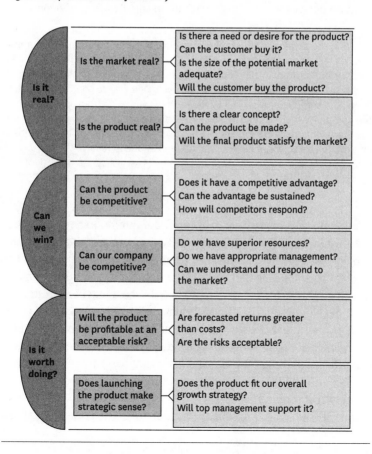

The Screening Team

PROJECT SCREENING TEAMS vary by company, type of initiative, and stage of development. Over the course of R-W-W screening, teams typically involve members from across functions, including R&D, marketing, and manufacturing. They should also work with senior managers who are familiar with the screen and have the expertise and the instincts to push dispassionately for accurate answers, particularly at each decision point during development. At the same time, however, these managers should be sympathetic and willing to provide the team with the resources to fill information gaps.

A critical job in managing the R-W-W process is preventing teams from regarding the screen as an obstacle to be overcome or circumvented. It's also important that the team not regard the screen as simply a go/no-go tool imposed by management—a potential threat to a favorite project. Such a misperception will subvert proper use of the screen as a learning tool for revealing dubious assumptions and identifying problems and solutions.

Because the members of the development team are both evaluators and advocates, the screen is vulnerable to misuse and manipulation. Team members' convictions about the merits of the project may lead them to make cursory evaluations if they fear that a deep assessment, including a frank voicing of doubts, might imperil the project. One way to avoid this pitfall is to enlist a credible outside facilitator, perhaps someone from another part of the company who has a solid new-product track record and no stake in the outcome. This person's job should be to unearth all the key uncertainties, information gaps, and differences of opinion and help resolve them.

from definitely yes to definitely no. A definite no to any of the first five fundamental questions typically leads to termination of the project, for obvious reasons. For example, if the consensus answer to *Can the product be competitive?* is a definite no, and the team can imagine no way to change it to a yes (or even a maybe), continuing with development is irrational. When a project has passed all other tests in the screen, however, and thus is a very good business bet, companies are sometimes more forgiving of a no to the sixth question, *Does launching the product make strategic sense?*

This article will delineate the screening process and demonstrate the depth of probing needed to arrive at valid answers. What follows is not, of course, a comprehensive guide to all the issues that might be raised by each question. Development teams can probe more or less deeply, as needed, at each decision point. (For more on team process, see the sidebar "The Screening Team.")

Is It Real?

Figuring out whether a market exists and whether a product can be made to satisfy that market are the first steps in screening a product concept. Those steps will indicate the degree of opportunity for any firm considering the potential market, so the inquiring company can assess how competitive the environment might be right from the start.

One might think that asking if the envisioned product is even a possibility should come before investigating the potential market. But establishing that the market is real takes precedence for two reasons: First, the robustness of a market is almost always less certain than the technological ability to make something. This is one of the messages of the risk matrix, which shows that the probability of a product failure becomes greater when the *market* is unfamiliar to the company than when the *product or technology* is unfamiliar. A company's ability to crystallize the market concept—the target segment and how the product can do a better job of meeting its needs—is far more important than how well the company fields a fundamentally new product or technology. In fact, research by Procter & Gamble suggests that 70% of product failures across most categories occur because companies misconstrue the market. New Coke is a classic market-concept failure; Netflix got the market concept right. In each case the outcome was determined by the company's understanding of the market, not its facility with the enabling technologies.

Second, establishing the nature of the market can head off a costly "technology push." This syndrome often afflicts companies that emphasize how to solve a problem rather than what problem should be solved or what customer desires need to be satisfied. Segway, with its Personal Transporter, and Motorola, with its Iridium satellite phone, both succumbed to technology push. Segway's PT was an ingenious way to gyroscopically stabilize a two-wheeled platform, but it didn't solve the mobility problems of any target market. The reasons for Iridium's demise are much debated, but one possibility is that mobile satellite services proved less able than terrestrial wireless roaming services to cost-effectively meet the needs of most travelers.

Whether the market and the product are real should dominate the screening dialogue early in the development process, especially for Big I innovations. In the case of little i innovations, a close alternative will already be on the market, which has been proved to be real.

Is the market real?

A market opportunity is real only when four conditions are satisfied: The proposed product will clearly meet a need or solve a problem better than available alternatives; customers are able to buy it; the potential market is big enough to be worth pursuing; and customers are willing to buy the product.

Is there a need or desire for the product? Unmet or poorly satisfied needs must be surfaced through market research using observational, ethnographic, and other tools to explore customers' behaviors, desires, motivations, and frustrations. Segway's poor showing is partly a market-research failure; the company didn't establish at the outset that consumers actually had a need for a self-balancing two-wheeled transporter.

Once a need has been identified, the next question is, *Can the customer buy it?* Even if the proposed product would satisfy a need and offer superior value, the market isn't real when there are objective barriers to purchasing it. Will budgetary constraints prevent customers from buying? (Teachers and school boards, for example, are always eager to invest in educational technologies but often can't find the funding.) Are there regulatory requirements that the new product may not meet? Are customers bound by contracts that would prevent them from switching to a new product? Could manufacturing or distribution problems prevent them from obtaining it?

The team next needs to ask, *Is the size of the potential market adequate?* It's dangerous to venture into a "trombone oil" market, where the product may provide distinctive value that satisfies a need, but the need is minuscule. A market opportunity isn't real unless there are enough potential buyers to warrant developing the product.

Finally, having established customers' need and ability to buy, the team must ask, *Will the customer buy the product?* Are there subjective barriers to purchasing it? If alternatives to the product exist, customers will evaluate them and consider, among other things, whether the new product delivers greater value in terms of features, capabilities, or cost. Improved value doesn't necessarily mean more capabilities, of course. Many Big I innovations, such as the Nintendo Wii, home defibrillators, and Salesforce.com's CRM software as a service, have prevailed by outperforming the incumbents on a few measures while being merely adequate on others. By the same token, some Big I innovations have stumbled because although they had novel capabilities, customers didn't find them superior to the incumbents.

Even when customers have a clear need or desire, old habits, the perception that a switch is too much trouble, or a belief that the purchase is risky can inhibit them. One company encountered just such a problem during the launch of a promising new epoxy for repairing machine parts during routine maintenance. Although the product could prevent costly shutdowns and thus offered unique value, the plant engineers and production managers at whom it was targeted vetoed its use. The engineers wanted more proof of the product's efficacy, while the production managers feared that it would damage equipment. Both groups were risk avoiders. A postmortem of the troubled launch revealed that maintenance people, unlike plant engineers and production managers, like to try new solutions. What's more, they could buy the product independently out of their own budgets, circumventing potential vetoes from higher up. The product was relaunched targeting maintenance and went on to become successful, but the delay was expensive and could have been avoided with better screening.

Customers may also be inhibited by a belief that the product will fail to deliver on its promise or that a better alternative might soon become available. Addressing this reluctance requires foresight into the possibilities of improvement among competitors. The prospects of third-generation (3G) mobile phones were dampened by enhancements in 2.5G phones, such as high-sensitivity antennae that made the incumbent technology perform much better.

Is the product real?

Once a company has established the reality of the market, it should look closely at the product concept and expand its examination of the intended market.

Is there a clear concept? Before development begins, the technology and performance requirements of the concept are usually poorly defined, and team members often have diverging ideas about the product's precise characteristics. This is the time to expose those ideas and identify exactly what is to be developed. As the project progresses and the team becomes immersed in market realities, the requirements should be clarified. This entails not only nailing down technical specifications but also evaluating the concept's legal, social, and environmental acceptability.

Can the product be made? If the concept is solid, the team must next explore whether a viable product is feasible. Could it be created with available technology and materials, or would it require a breakthrough of some sort? If the product can be made, can it be produced and delivered cost-effectively, or would it be so expensive that potential customers would shun it? Feasibility also requires either that a value chain for the proposed product exists or that it can be easily and affordably developed, and that de facto technology standards (such as those ensuring compatibility among products) can be met.

Some years ago the R-W-W screen was used to evaluate a radical proposal to build nuclear power-generating stations on enormous floating platforms moored offshore. Power companies were drawn to the idea, because it solved both cooling and not-in-my-backyard problems. But the team addressing the *Is the product real?* stage of the process found that the inevitable flexing of the giant platforms would lead to metal fatigue and joint wear in pumps and turbines. Since this problem was deemed insurmountable, the team concluded that absent some technological breakthrough, the no answer to the feasibility question could never become even a maybe, and development was halted.

Will the final product satisfy the market? During development, trade-offs are made in performance attributes; unforeseen technical, manufacturing, or systems problems arise; and features are modified. At each such turn in the road, a product designed to meet customer expectations may lose some of its potential appeal. Failure to monitor these shifts can result in the launch of an offering that looked great on the drawing board but falls flat in the marketplace.

Can We Win?

After determining that the market and the product are both real, the project team must assess the company's ability to gain and hold an adequate share of the market. Simply finding a real opportunity doesn't guarantee success: The more real the opportunity, the more likely it is that hungry competitors are eyeing it. And if the market is already established, incumbents will defend their positions by copying or leapfrogging any innovations.

Two of the top three reasons for new-product failures, as revealed by audits, would have been exposed by the *Can we win?* analysis: Either the new product didn't achieve its market-share goals, or prices dropped much faster than expected. (The third reason is that the market was smaller, or grew more slowly, than expected.)

The questions at this stage of the R-W-W screening carefully distinguish between the offering's ability to succeed in the marketplace and the company's capacity—through resources and management talent—to help it do so.

Can the product be competitive?

Customers will choose one product over alternatives if it's perceived as delivering superior value with some combination of benefits such as better features, lower life-cycle cost, and reduced risk. The team must assess all sources of perceived value for a given product and consider the question *Does it have a competitive advantage?* (Here the customer research that informed the team's evaluation of whether the market and the product were real should be drawn on and extended as needed.) Can someone else's offering provide customers with the same results or benefits? One company's promising laminate technology, for instance, had intrigued technical experts, but the launch failed because the customers' manufacturing people had found other, cheaper ways to achieve the same improvement. The team should also consider whether the product offers additional tangible advantages—such as lifetime cost savings, greater safety, higher quality, and lower maintenance or support needs—or intangible benefits, such as greater social acceptability (think of hybrid cars and synthetic-fur coats) and the promise of reduced risk that is implicit in a trusted brand name.

Can the advantage be sustained? Competitive advantage is only as good as the company's ability to keep imitators at bay. The first line of defense is patents. The project team should evaluate the relevance of its existing patents to the product in development and decide what additional patents may be needed to protect related intellectual property. It should ask whether a competitor could reverse engineer the product or otherwise circumvent patents that are essential to the product's success. If maintaining advantage lies in tacit organizational knowledge, can that knowledge be protected? For example, how can the company ensure that the people who have it will stay? What other barriers to imitation are possible? Can the company lock up scarce resources or enter into exclusive supply contracts?

Consider the case of 3M's computer privacy screen. Although the company's microlouver technology promised unique privacy benefits, its high price threatened to limit sales to a small market niche, making the project's status uncertain. An R-W-W screening, however, revealed that the technology was aggressively patented, so no competitor could imitate its performance. It also clarified an opportunity in adjacent markets for antiglare filters for computers. Armed with these insights, 3M used the technology to launch a full line of privacy and antiglare screens while leveraging its brand equity and sales presence in the office-products market. Five years later the product line formed the basis of one of 3M's fastest-growing businesses.

How will competitors respond? Assuming that patent protection is (or will be) in place, the project team needs to investigate competitive threats that patents can't deflect. A good place to start is a "red team" exercise: If we were going to attack our own product, what vulnerabilities would we find? How can we reduce them? A common error companies make is to assume that competitors will stand still while the new entrant fine-tunes its product prior to launch. Thus the team must consider what competing products will look like when the offering is introduced, how competitors may react after the launch, and how the company could respond. Finally, the team should examine the possible effects of this competitive interplay on prices. Would the product survive a sustained price war?

Can our company be competitive?

After establishing that the offering can win, the team must determine whether or not the company's resources, management, and market insight are better than those of the competition. If not, it may be impossible to sustain advantage, no matter how good the product.

Do we have superior resources? The odds of success increase markedly when a company has or can get resources that both enhance customers' perception of the new product's value and surpass those of competitors. Superior engineering, service delivery, logistics, or brand equity can give a new product an edge by better meeting customers' expectations. The European no-frills airline easyJet, for example, has successfully expanded into cruises and car rentals by leveraging its ability to blend convenience, low cost, and market-appropriate branding to appeal to small-business people and other price-sensitive travelers.

If the company doesn't have superior resources, addressing the deficiency is often straightforward. When the U.S. market leader for high-efficiency lighting products wanted to expand into the local-government market, for example, it recognized two barriers: The company was unknown to the buyers, and it had no experience with the competitive bidding process they used. It overcame these problems by hiring people who were skilled at analyzing competitors, anticipating their likely bids, and writing proposals. Some of these people came from the competition, which put the company's rivals at a disadvantage.

Sometimes, though, deficiencies are more difficult to overcome, as is the case with brand equity. As part of its inquiry into resources, the project team must ask whether the company's brand provides—or denies—permission to enter the market. The 3M name gave a big boost to the privacy screen because it is strongly associated with high-quality, innovative office supplies—whereas the McDonald's name couldn't stretch to include pizza. Had the company's management asked whether its brand equity was both relevant and superior to that of the competition—such as Papa Gino's—the answer would have been equivocal at best.

Do we have appropriate management? Here the team must examine whether the organization has direct or related experience with the market, whether its development-process skills are appropriate for the scale and complexity of the project, and whether the project both fits company culture and has a suitable champion. Success requires a passionate cheerleader who will energize the team, sell the vision to senior management, and overcome skepticism or adversity along the way. But because enthusiasm can blind champions to potentially crippling faults and lead to a biased search for evidence that confirms a project's viability, their advocacy must be constructively challenged throughout the screening process.

Can we understand and respond to the market? Successful product development requires a mastery of market-research tools, an openness to customer insights, and the ability to share them with development-team members. Repeatedly seeking the feedback of potential customers to refine concepts, prototypes, and pricing ensures that products won't have to be recycled through the development process to fix deficiencies.

Most companies wait until after development to figure out how to price the new product—and then sometimes discover that customers won't pay. Procter & Gamble avoids this problem by including pricing research early in the development process. It also asks customers to actually buy products in development. Their answers to *whether* they would buy are not always reliable predictors of future purchasing behavior.

Is It Worth Doing?

Just because a project can pass the tests up to this point doesn't mean it is worth pursuing. The final stage of the screening provides a more rigorous analysis of financial and strategic value.

Will the product be profitable at an acceptable risk?

Few products launch unless top management is persuaded that the answer to *Are forecasted returns greater than costs?* is definitely yes. This requires projecting the timing and amount of capital outlays, marketing expenses, costs, and margins; applying time to breakeven, cash flow, net present value, and other standard financial-performance measures; and estimating the profitability and cash flow from both aggressive and cautious launch plans. Financial projections should also include the cost of product extensions and enhancements needed to keep ahead of the competition.

Forecasts of financial returns from new products are notoriously unreliable. Project managers know they are competing with other worthy projects for scarce resources and don't want theirs to be at a disadvantage. So it is not surprising that project teams' financial reports usually meet upper management's financial-performance requirements. Given the susceptibility of financial forecasts to manipulation, overconfidence, and bias, executives should depend on rigorous answers to the prior questions in the screen for their conclusions about profitability.

Are the risks acceptable? A forecast's riskiness can be initially assessed with a standard sensitivity test: How will small changes in price, market share, and launch timing affect cash flows and breakeven points? A big change in financial results stemming from a small one in input assumptions indicates a high degree of risk. The financial analysis should consider opportunity costs: Committing resources to one project may hamper the development of others.

To understand risk at a deeper level, consider all the potential causes of product failure that have been unearthed by the R-W-W screen and devise ways to mitigate them—such as partnering with a company that has market or technology expertise your firm lacks.

Does launching the product make strategic sense?

Even when a market and a concept are real, the product and the company could win, and the project would be profitable, it may not make strategic sense to launch. To evaluate the strategic rationale for development, the project team should ask two more questions.

Does the product fit our overall growth strategy? In other words, will it enhance the company's capabilities by, for example, driving the expansion of manufacturing, logistics, or other functions? Will it have a positive or a negative impact on brand equity? Will it cannibalize or improve sales of the company's existing products? (If the former, is it better to cannibalize one's own products than to lose sales to competitors?) Will it enhance or harm relationships with stakeholders—dealers, distributors, regulators, and so forth? Does the project create opportunities for follow-on business or new markets that would not be possible otherwise? (Such an opportunity helped 3M decide to launch its privacy screen: The product had only a modest market on its own, but the launch opened up a much bigger market for antiglare filters.) These questions can serve as a starting point for what must be a thorough evaluation of the product's strategic fit. A discouraging answer to just one of them shouldn't kill a project outright, but if the overall results suggest that a project makes little strategic sense, the launch is probably ill-advised.

Will top management support it? It's certainly encouraging for a development team when management commits to the initial concept. But the ultimate success of a project is better assured if management signs on because the project's assumptions can withstand the rigorous challenges of the R-W-W screen.

Notes

1. Robert G. Cooper, "Your NPD Portfolio May Be Harmful to Your Business Health," *PDMA Visions,* April 2005.

2. W. Chan Kim and Renée Mauborgne, "Strategy, Value Innovation, and the Knowledge Economy," *Sloan Management Review,* Spring 1999.

Adapted from an article originally published in December 2007. Reprint R07125

Superforecasting

How to Upgrade Your Company's Judgment. *by Paul J. H. Schoemaker and Philip E. Tetlock*

IMAGINE THAT YOU COULD DRAMATICALLY IMPROVE your firm's forecasting ability, but to do so you'd have to expose just how unreliable its predictions—and the people making them—really are. That's exactly what the U.S. intelligence community did, with dramatic results. Back in October 2002, the National Intelligence Council issued its official opinion that Iraq possessed chemical and biological weapons and was actively producing more weapons of mass destruction. Of course, that judgment proved colossally wrong. Shaken by its intelligence failure, the $50 billion bureaucracy set out to determine how it could do better in the future, realizing that the process might reveal glaring organizational deficiencies.

The resulting research program included a large-scale, multiyear prediction tournament, co-led by one of us (Phil), called the Good Judgment Project. The series of contests, which pitted thousands of amateurs against seasoned intelligence analysts, generated three surprising insights: First, talented generalists often outperform specialists in making forecasts. Second, carefully crafted training can enhance predictive acumen. And third, well-run teams can outperform individuals. These findings have important implications for the way organizations and businesses forecast uncertain outcomes, such as how a competitor will respond to a new-product launch,

About the Good Judgment Project

IN 2011, PHILIP TETLOCK teamed up with Barbara Mellers, of the Wharton School, to launch the Good Judgment Project. The goal was to determine whether some people are naturally better than others at prediction and whether prediction performance could be enhanced. The GJP was one of five academic research teams that competed in an innovative tournament funded by the Intelligence Advanced Research Projects Activity (IARPA), in which forecasters were challenged to answer the types of geopolitical and economic questions that U.S. intelligence agencies pose to their analysts.

The IARPA initiative ran from 2011 to 2015 and recruited more than 25,000 forecasters who made well over a million predictions on topics ranging from whether Greece would exit the eurozone to the likelihood of a leadership turnover in Russia to the risk of a financial panic in China. The GJP decisively won the tournament—besting even the intelligence community's own analysts.

how much revenue a promotion will generate, or whether prospective hires will perform well.

The approach we'll describe here for building an ever-improving organizational forecasting capability is not a cookbook that offers proven recipes for success. Many of the principles are fairly new and have only recently been applied in business settings. However, our research shows that they can help leaders discover and nurture their organizations' best predictive capabilities wherever they may reside.

Find the Sweet Spot

Companies and individuals are notoriously inept at judging the likelihood of uncertain events, as studies show all too well. Getting judgments wrong, of course, can have serious consequences. Steve Ballmer's prognostication in 2007 that "there's no chance that the iPhone is going to get any significant market share" left Microsoft with no room to consider alternative scenarios. But improving a firm's forecasting competence even a little can yield a competitive advantage. A company that is right three times out of five on its judgment calls is going to have an ever-increasing edge on a competitor that gets them right only two times out of five.

Idea in Brief

The Problem

Organizations and individuals are notoriously poor at judging the likelihood of uncertain events. Predictions are often colored by the forecaster's susceptibility to cognitive biases, desire to influence others, and concerns about reputation. Getting judgments wrong can of course have serious consequences.

The Research

On the basis of research involving 25,000 forecasters and a million predictions, the authors identified a set of practices that can improve companies' prediction capability: training in the basics of statistics and biases; debating forecasts in teams; and tracking performance and giving rapid feedback.

In Practice

To improve prediction capability, companies should keep real-time accounts of how their top teams make judgments, including underlying assumptions, data sources, external events, and so on. Keys to success include requiring frequent, precise predictions and measuring accuracy for comparison.

Before we discuss how an organization can build a predictive edge, let's look at the types of judgments that are most amenable to improvement—and those not worth focusing on. We can dispense with predictions that are either entirely straightforward or seemingly impossible. Consider issues that are highly predictable: You know where the hands of your clock will be five hours from now; life insurance companies can reliably set premiums on the basis of updated mortality tables. For issues that can be predicted with great accuracy using econometric and operations-research tools, there is no advantage to be gained by developing subjective judgment skills in those areas: The data speaks loud and clear.

At the other end of the spectrum, we find issues that are complex, poorly understood, and tough to quantify, such as the patterns of clouds on a given day or when the next game-changing technology will pop out of a garage in Silicon Valley. Here, too, there's little advantage in investing resources in systematically improving judgment: The problems are just too hard to crack.

The sweet spot that companies should focus on is forecasts for which some data, logic, and analysis can be used but seasoned judgment and careful questioning also play key roles. Predicting the commercial potential of drugs in clinical trials requires scientific expertise as well as business judgment. Assessors of acquisition candidates draw on formal scoring models, but they must also gauge intangibles such as cultural fit, the chemistry among leaders, and the likelihood that anticipated synergies will actually materialize.

Consider the experience of a UK bank that lost a great deal of money in the early 1990s by lending to U.S. cable companies that were hot but then tanked. The chief lending officer conducted an audit of these presumed lending errors, analyzing the types of loans made, the characteristics of clients and loan officers involved, the incentives at play, and other factors. She scored the bad loans on each factor and then ran an analysis to see which ones best explained the variance in the amounts lost. In cases where the losses were substantial, she found problems in the underwriting process that resulted in loans to clients with poor financial health or no prior relationship with the bank—issues for which expertise and judgment were important. The bank was able to make targeted improvements that boosted performance and minimized losses.

On the basis of our research and consulting experience, we have identified a set of practices that leaders can apply to improve their firms' judgment in this middle ground. Our recommendations focus on improving individuals' forecasting ability through training; using teams to boost accuracy; and tracking prediction performance and providing rapid feedback. The general approaches we describe should of course be tailored to each organization and evolve as the firm learns what works in which circumstances.

Train for Good Judgment

Most predictions made in companies, whether they concern project budgets, sales forecasts, or the performance of potential hires or acquisitions, are not the result of cold calculus. They are colored by the forecaster's understanding of basic statistical arguments, susceptibility to cognitive biases, desire to influence others' thinking, and concerns about reputation. Indeed, predictions are often intentionally vague to maximize wiggle room should they prove wrong. The good news is that training in reasoning and debiasing can reliably strengthen a firm's forecasting competence. The Good Judgment Project demonstrated that as little as one hour of training improved forecasting accuracy by about 14% over the course of a year. (See the exhibit "How training and teams improve prediction.")

Learn the basics

Basic reasoning errors (such as believing that a coin that has landed heads three times in a row is likelier to land tails on the next flip) take a toll on prediction accuracy. So it's essential that companies lay a foundation of forecasting basics: The GJP's training in probability concepts such as regression to the mean and Bayesian revision (updating a probability estimate in light of new data), for example, boosted participants' accuracy measurably. Companies should also require that forecasts include a precise definition of what is to be predicted (say, the chance that a potential hire will meet her sales targets) and the time frame involved (one year, for example). The prediction itself must be expressed as a numeric probability so that it can be precisely scored for accuracy later. That means asserting that one is "80% confident," rather than "fairly sure," that the prospective employee will meet her targets.

Understand cognitive biases

Cognitive biases are widely known to skew judgment, and some have particularly pernicious effects on forecasting. They lead people to follow the crowd, to look for information that confirms their views, and to strive to prove just how right they are. It's a tall order to debias human judgment, but the GJP has had some success in raising participants' awareness of key biases that compromise forecasting. For example, the project trained beginners to watch out for confirmation bias that can create false confidence, and to give due weight to evidence that challenges their conclusions. And it reminded trainees to not look at problems in isolation but, rather, take what Nobel laureate Daniel Kahneman calls "the outside view." For instance, in predicting how long a project will take to complete, trainees were counseled to first ask how long it typically takes to complete similar projects, to avoid underestimating the time needed.

Training can also help people understand the psychological factors that lead to biased probability estimates, such as the tendency to rely on flawed intuition in lieu of careful analysis. Statistical intuitions are notoriously susceptible to illusions and superstition. Stock market analysts may see patterns in the data that have no statistical basis, and sports fans often regard basketball free-throw streaks, or "hot hands," as evidence of extraordinary new capability when in fact they're witnessing a mirage caused by capricious variations in a small sample size.

Another technique for making people aware of the psychological biases underlying skewed estimates is to give them "confidence quizzes." Participants are asked for range estimates about general-interest questions (such as "How old was Martin Luther King Jr. when he died?") or company-specific ones (such as "How much federal tax did our firm pay in the past year?"). The predictors' task is to give their best guess in the form of a range and assign a degree of confidence to it; for example, one might guess with 90% confidence that Dr. King was between 40 and 55 when he was assassinated (he was 39). The aim is to measure not participants' domain-specific knowledge, but, rather, how well they know what they don't know. As Will Rogers wryly noted: "It is not what we don't know that gets us into trouble; it is what we know that ain't so." Participants commonly discover that half or more of their 90% confidence ranges don't contain the true answer.

Again, there's no one-size-fits-all remedy for avoiding these systematic errors; companies should tailor training programs to their circumstances. Susquehanna International Group, a privately held global quantitative trading firm, has its own idiosyncratic approach. Founded in 1987 by poker aficionados, the company, which transacts more than a billion dollars in trades a year, requires new hires to play lots of poker—on company time. In the process, trainees learn about cognitive traps, emotional influences such as wishful thinking, behavioral game theory, and, of course, options theory, arbitrage, and foreign exchange and trading regulations. The poker-playing exercises sensitize the trainees to the value of thinking in probability terms, focusing on information asymmetry (what the opponent might know that I don't), learning when to fold a bad hand, and defining success not as winning each round but as making the most of the hand you are dealt.

Companies should also engage in customized training that focuses on narrower prediction domains, such as sales and R&D, or areas where past performance has been especially poor. If your sales team is prone to hubris, that bias can be systematically addressed. Such tailored programs are more challenging to develop and run than general ones, but because they are targeted, they often yield greater benefits.

Build the Right Kind of Teams

Assembling forecasters into teams is an effective way to improve forecasts. In the Good Judgment Project, several hundred forecasters were randomly assigned to work alone and several hundred to work collaboratively in teams. In each of the four years of the IARAP tournament, the forecasters working in teams outperformed those who worked alone. Of course, to achieve good results, teams must be deftly managed and have certain distinctive features.

Composition

The forecasters who do the best in GJP tournaments are brutally honest about the source of their success, appreciating that they may have gotten a prediction right despite (not because of) their analysis. They are cautious, humble, open-minded, analytical—and good with numbers. (See the sidebar "Who Are These Superforecasters?") In assembling teams, companies should look for natural forecasters who show an alertness to bias, a knack for sound reasoning, and a respect for data.

How training and teams improve prediction

The Good Judgment Project tracked the accuracy of participants' forecasts about economic and geopolitical events. The control group, made up of motivated volunteers, received no training about the biases that can plague forecasters. Its members performed at about the same level as most employees in high-quality companies—perhaps even better, since they were self-selected, competitive individuals. The second group benefited from training on biases and how to overcome them. Teams of trained individuals who debated their forecasts (usually virtually) performed even better. When the best forecasters were culled over successive rounds into an elite group of superforecasters, their predictions were nearly twice as accurate as those made by untrained forecasters—representing a huge opportunity for companies.

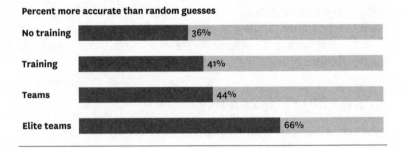

Percent more accurate than random guesses

No training	36%
Training	41%
Teams	44%
Elite teams	66%

It's also important that forecasting teams be intellectually diverse. At least one member should have domain expertise (a finance professional on a budget forecasting team, for example), but nonexperts are essential too—particularly ones who won't shy away from challenging the presumed experts. Don't underestimate these generalists. In the GJP contests, nonexpert civilian forecasters often beat trained intelligence analysts at their own game.

Diverging, evaluating, and converging

Whether a team is making a forecast about a single event (such as the likelihood of a U.S. recession two years from now) or making recurring predictions (such as the risk each year of recession in an array of countries), a successful team needs to manage three phases well:

Who Are These Superforecasters?

THE GOOD JUDGMENT PROJECT identified the traits shared by the best-performing forecasters in the Intelligence Advanced Research Projects Activity tournament. A public tournament is ongoing at gjopen.com; join to see if you have what it takes.

Philosophical approach and outlook

Cautious: They understand that few things are certain

Humble: They appreciate their limits

Nondeterministic: They don't assume that what happens is meant to be

---

Abilities and thinking style

Open-minded: They see beliefs as hypotheses to be tested

Inquiring: They are intellectually curious and enjoy mental challenges

Reflective: They are introspective and self-critical

Numerate: They are comfortable with numbers

Methods of forecasting

Pragmatic: They are not wedded to any one idea or agenda

Analytical: They consider other views

Synthesizing: They blend diverse views into their own

Probability-focused: They judge the probability of events not as certain or uncertain but as more or less likely

Thoughtful updaters: They change their minds when new facts warrant it

Intuitive shrinks: They are aware of their cognitive and emotional biases

---

Work ethic

Improvement-minded: They strive to get better

Tenacious: They stick with a problem for as long as needed

---

a diverging phase, in which the issue, assumptions, and approaches to finding an answer are explored from multiple angles; an evaluating phase, which includes time for productive disagreement; and a converging phase, when the team settles on a prediction. In each of these phases, learning and progress are fastest when questions are focused and feedback is frequent.

The diverging and evaluating phases are essential; if they are cursory or ignored, the team develops tunnel vision—focusing too narrowly and quickly locking into a wrong answer—and prediction quality suffers. The right norms can help prevent this, including a focus on gathering new information and testing assumptions relevant to the forecasts. Teams must also focus on neutralizing a common prediction error called anchoring, wherein an early—and possibly ill-advised—estimate skews subsequent opinions far too long. This often happens unconsciously because easily available numbers serve as convenient starting points. (Even random numbers, when used in an initial estimate, have been shown to anchor people's final judgments.)

One of us (Paul) ran an experiment with University of Chicago MBA subjects that demonstrated the impact of divergent exploration on the path to a final prediction. In one test, subjects in the control group were asked to estimate how many gold medals the U.S. would win relative to another top country in the next summer Olympics and to provide their 90% confidence ranges around these estimates. The other group was asked to first sketch out various reasons why the ratio of medals might be lower or higher than in years past and then make an estimate. This group naturally thought back to terrorist attacks and boycotts, and considered other factors that might influence the outcome, from illness to improved training to performance-enhancing drugs. As a consequence of this divergent thinking, this group's ranges were significantly wider than the control group's, often by more than half. In general, wider ranges reflect more carefully weighed predictions; narrow ranges commonly indicate overconfident—and often less accurate—forecasts.

Trust

Finally, trust among members of any team is required for good outcomes. It is particularly critical for prediction teams because of the nature of the work. Teams that are predicting the success or failure of a new acquisition, or handicapping the odds of successfully divesting a part of the business, may reach conclusions that raise turf issues or threaten egos and reputations. They are also likely to expose areas of the firm, and perhaps individuals, with poor forecasting abilities. To ensure that forecasters share their best thinking, members must trust one another and trust that leadership will defend their work and protect their jobs and reputations. Few things chill a forecasting team faster than a sense that its conclusions could threaten the team itself.

Track Performance and Give Feedback

Our work on the Good Judgment Project and with a range of companies shows that tracking prediction outcomes and providing timely feedback is essential to improving forecasting performance.

Consider U.S. weather forecasters, who, though much maligned, excel at what they do. When they say there's a 30% chance of rain, 30% of the time it rains on those days, on average. Key to their superior performance is that they receive timely, continual, and unambiguous feedback about their accuracy, which is often tied to their performance reviews. Bridge players, internal auditors, and oil geologists also shine at prediction thanks in part to robust feedback and incentives for improvement.

The purest measure for the accuracy of predictions and tracking them over time is the Brier score. It allows companies to make direct, statistically reliable comparisons among forecasters across a series of predictions. Over time, the scores reveal those who excel, be they individuals, members of a team, or entire teams competing with others. (See the sidebar "Brier Scores Reveal Your Best—and Worst—Predictors.")

But simply knowing a team's score does little to improve performance; you have to track the process it used as well. It's important to audit why outcomes were achieved—good or bad—so that you can learn from them. Some audits may reveal that certain process steps led to a good or a bad prediction. Others may show that a forecast was correct despite a faulty rationale (that is, it was lucky), or that a forecast was wrong because of unusual circumstances rather than a flawed analysis. For example, a retailer may make very accurate forecasts of how many customers will visit a store on a given day,

Brier Scores Reveal Your Best—and Worst—Predictors

IT'S IMPORTANT THAT FORECASTERS make precise estimates of probability—for example, pegging at 80% the likelihood that their firm will sell between 9,000 and 11,000 units of a new product in the first quarter. That way, the predictions can be analyzed and compared using a method called Brier scoring, allowing managers to reliably rank forecasters on the basis of skill.

Brier scores are calculated by squaring the difference between a probability prediction and the actual outcome, scored as 1 if the event happened and 0 if not. For example, if a forecaster assigns a 0.9 probability (a 90% confidence level) that the firm will exceed a sales target and the firm then does, her Brier score for that forecast is:

$$(0.9 - 1)^2, \text{ or } 0.01.$$

If the firm misses the target, her score is:

$$(0.9 - 0)^2, \text{ or } 0.81.$$

The closer to zero the score is, the smaller the forecast error and the better the prediction.

Brier scoring makes it readily apparent who's good at forecasting and who isn't. By enabling direct comparison among forecasters, the tool encourages thoughtful analysis while exposing "shooting from the hip" and biased prognostications.

---

but if a black-swan event—say, a bomb threat—closes the store, its forecast for that day will be badly off. Its Brier score would indicate poor performance, but a process audit would show that bad luck, not bad process, accounted for the outlying score.

Gauging group dynamics is also a critical part of the process audit. No amount of good data and by-the-book forecasting can overcome flawed team dynamics. Consider the discussions that took place between NASA and engineering contractor Morton Thiokol before the doomed launch of the space shuttle *Challenger* in 1986. At first, Thiokol engineers advised against the launch, concerned that cold temperatures could compromise the O-rings that sealed the rocket boosters' joints. They predicted a much higher than usual chance of failure because of the temperature. Ultimately, and tragically, Thiokol reversed its stance.

The engineers' analysis was good; the organizational process was flawed. A reconstruction of the events that day, based on congressional hearings, revealed the interwoven conditions that compromised the forecast: time pressure, directive leadership, failure to fully explore alternate views, silencing of dissenters, and a sense of infallibility (after all, 24 previous flights had gone well).

To avoid such catastrophes—and to replicate successes—companies should systematically collect real-time accounts of how their top teams make judgments, keeping records of assumptions made, data used, experts consulted, external events, and so on. Videos or transcripts of meetings can be used to analyze process; asking forecasters to record their own process may also offer important insights. Recall Susquehanna International Group, which trains its traders to play poker. Those traders are required to document their rationale for entering or exiting a trade before making a transaction. They are asked to consider key questions: What information might others have that you don't that might affect the trade? What cognitive traps might skew your judgment on this transaction? Why do you believe the firm has an edge on this trade? Susquehanna further emphasizes the importance of process by pegging traders' bonuses not just to the outcome of individual trades but also to whether the underlying analytic process was sound.

Well-run audits can reveal post facto whether forecasters coalesced around a bad anchor, framed the problem poorly, overlooked an important insight, or failed to engage (or even muzzled) team members with dissenting views. Likewise, they can highlight the process steps that led to good forecasts and thereby provide other teams with best practices for improving predictions.

Each of the methods we've described—training, team building, tracking, and talent spotting—is essential to good forecasting. The approach must be customized across businesses, and no firm, to our knowledge, has yet mastered them all to create a fully integrated program. This presents a great opportunity for companies that take the lead—particularly those with a culture of organizational innovation and those who embrace the kind of experimentation the intelligence community did.

But companies will capture this advantage only if respected leaders champion the effort, by broadcasting an openness to trial and error, a willingness to ruffle feathers, and a readiness to expose "what we know that ain't so" in order to hone the firm's predictive edge.

Originally published in May 2016. Reprint R1605E

Managing 21st-Century Political Risk

by Condoleezza Rice and Amy Zegart

IN 2010, Gabriela Cowperthwaite read a news article that changed her life. It described how an orca whale had killed a trainer during a show at SeaWorld in Orlando. Cowperthwaite, a Los Angeles filmmaker who liked taking her twins to see orcas at the San Diego SeaWorld, spent the next two years making an investigative documentary, *Blackfish*, which depicted how the theme parks' treatment of orcas harmed both the animals and their human trainers. The film cost just $76,000 to produce. Yet it quickly went viral, capturing the attention of celebrities and animal rights groups. Public pressure on SeaWorld mounted. Corporations cut sponsorship ties, regulators opened investigations into the parks' safety practices, and lawmakers proposed a ban on breeding orcas in captivity. Eighteen months after the release of *Blackfish*, SeaWorld's stock price had plunged 60%, and CEO Jim Atchison announced that he was resigning. By 2018, SeaWorld's stock still had not recovered—all because one woman had read a story about orcas and made a low-budget film.

Until recently, political risk was relatively easy to understand. More often than not, it involved dictators who suddenly seized foreign assets for their own domestic agendas, like Venezuela's Hugo Chávez. Today expropriating leaders are far less common than they used to be. And although national governments are still the main arbiters of the business environment, a great deal of the political risk within and across countries now comes from other players: individuals wielding cell phones, local officials issuing city ordinances, terrorists detonating truck bombs, UN officials administering sanctions, and many more. Events in far-flung places affect businesses around the world at dizzying speed. Anti-Chinese protests in Vietnam create clothing stock-outs in America. Civil war in Syria fuels a refugee crisis and terrorist attacks in Europe, leaving the tourism industry shaken. A North Korean dictator launches a cyberattack on a Hollywood movie studio. We live in a new world of political risk.

For companies, 21st-century political risk is essentially the probability that a political action will significantly affect their business—whether positively or negatively. This definition is more radical than it sounds. We chose the phrase "political action," not "government action," to highlight the growing role of risk generators outside the usual places like capitals, army barracks, and party headquarters. These days, political activities that affect business are happening almost everywhere—inside homes, on the streets, and in the cloud; in chat rooms, dorm rooms, and boardrooms; in neighborhood bars and summit sidebars. Companies that want a competitive edge need to manage the potential impact of this widening array of global political actors.

Considered in isolation, many 21st-century political risks seem like low-probability events. If you're American, the chance that you'll be killed by a foreign-born terrorist is about one in 45,000—far more remote than your odds of dying from a heat wave or by choking on food. Unlike *Blackfish,* most social-activism documentaries don't become viral sensations. Cumulative risk is a different matter, however, and is easy to underestimate. While the probability that a single political risk will affect a company's business in a particular city tomorrow may be low, the probability that over time *some* political risk somewhere in the world will significantly affect its business is surprisingly high. Add up a string of rare events, and you'll find that the overall incidence is not so rare after all.

The good news is that while political risk has grown complex, effectively managing it remains fairly straightforward. Organizations can

Idea in Brief

The Challenge

Political risk was once fairly easy to understand; more often than not, it involved dictators who suddenly seized foreign assets. But increasingly it comes from other actors: people making videos on their cell phones, city officials issuing ordinances, terrorists detonating truck bombs, and many more.

Complicating Factors

First, the end of the Cold War superpower rivalry has made the geopolitical landscape more crowded and uncertain. Second, longer, leaner supply chains have left companies more vulnerable to disruptions in faraway places. Finally, new technologies mean that social activism isn't just for social activists anymore. Bystanders can post videos that go viral and cause significant political damage to companies.

The Solution

Organizations that excel at risk management have four core competencies: understanding, analyzing, mitigating, and responding to political risks. A series of questions can help executives identify gaps in each area and increase their ability to get ahead of and minimize risk.

get ahead by getting the basics right. Building on existing best practices and drawing on our own leadership experiences and research, we have identified four core competencies of organizations that excel at risk management—and a series of questions that can help executives identify gaps in their organizations' ability to operate in an era of increasing global insecurity.

The New Forces behind Political Risk

Three megatrends are transforming the landscape for political risk: dramatic changes in politics since the end of the Cold War, supply chain innovations, and the tech revolution.

Politics

Companies today operate in the most complicated international political environment in modern history. During the Cold War, superpower rivalry between the United States and the Soviet Union set relatively

Ten Types of Political Risk

IN THE TABLE BELOW, we summarize the major types of political risk that companies face in the 21st century. Our definition of political risk goes beyond the probability that an action by government officials could affect a company in significant ways; to us it includes the impact of political actions by a wide range of people and organizations. We've chosen to exclude climate change and purely economic risks, however. Climate change is a major global challenge, but we view it as more of a risk multiplier than a separate risk category. It can trigger political actions, from social activism and new regulations to civil wars and interstate conflicts—all risks that our list covers. And we left out economic risks because most businesses already consider them routinely, examining indicators such as inflation, labor markets, growth rates, and per capita income across markets.

Geopolitics	Interstate wars, great power shifts, multilateral economic sanctions, and interventions
Internal conflict	Social unrest, ethnic violence, migration, nationalism, separatism, federalism, civil wars, coups, and revolutions
Laws, regulations, policies	Changes in foreign ownership rules, taxation, environmental regulations, and national laws
Breaches of contract	Government reneging on contracts, including expropriations and politically motivated credit defaults
Corruption	Discriminatory taxation and systemic bribery
Extraterritorial reach	Unilateral sanctions and criminal investigations and prosecutions
Natural resource manipulation	Politically motivated changes to the supplies of energy and rare earth minerals
Social activism	Events or opinions that go viral, facilitating collective action
Terrorism	Politically motivated threats or violence against persons and property
Cyberthreats	Theft or destruction of intellectual property; espionage; extortion; and massive disruption of companies, industries, governments, and societies

clear dividing lines between adversaries and allies. Trade politics and security politics were sharply delineated, too. The world was largely split between Western capitalist markets and the command economies of the Soviet bloc. Arms control treaties involved the Soviets, but global trade negotiations did not. Today's landscape is much more crowded and uncertain—filled with rising states, declining states, failed states, rogue states, and nonstate actors like terrorist groups and cybercriminals. And security isn't just about security anymore; international economic issues are often tightly connected to security policy and politics.

When Condi was secretary of state, she watched in dismay as Dubai Ports World, an award-winning port management company owned by the government of the United Arab Emirates, was forced to transfer its ownership of U.S.-based shipping terminal operations to an American entity following a public backlash. Although the UAE was a staunch U.S. ally and a thorough U.S. government review had found no security concerns with the deal, Americans heard the words "Arabs" and "ports," and in the aftermath of 9/11, that was enough to make Dubai Ports World's operations in the U.S. untenable—even in one of the staunchest pro-market economies in the world.

Supply chains

The growing efficiency of supply chains is unlocking enormous value for companies. Even very small businesses can now take advantage of lower offshore wages, low shipping costs, and better inventory management. But there is a dark side to the supply chain revolution: Longer, leaner global supply chains leave companies more vulnerable to disruptions in faraway places.

As companies extend their overseas supplier relationships in search of improved margins, customization, and speed, the chances rise that a political action will disrupt the distribution of goods and services to their customers. When China moved an offshore oil rig into Vietnam's exclusive economic zone in 2014, anti-Chinese protests erupted in Vietnam. Suppliers of Li & Fung, one of the world's largest wholesale providers of clothing and toys, were forced to close their Vietnamese factories for a week, slowing delivery of goods to

Guiding Questions for Managing Political Risk

EFFECTIVE RISK MANAGEMENT REQUIRES four core competencies: understanding risks, analyzing risks, mitigating risks, and responding to crises. In each competency, three questions will help identify gaps and areas for improvement.

Understand	Analyze	Mitigate	Respond
What is my organization's political risk appetite?	How can we get good information about the political risks we face?	How can we reduce exposure to the political risks we have identified?	Are we capitalizing on near misses?
Is there a shared understanding of our risk appetite?	How can we ensure rigorous analysis?	Do we have a good system and team in place for timely warning and action?	Are we reacting effectively to crises?
How can we reduce blind spots?	How can we integrate political risk analysis into business decisions?	How can we limit the damage when something bad happens?	Are we developing mechanisms for continuous learning?

the United States. What had begun as a conflict over disputed territorial waters in Southeast Asia quickly emptied store shelves in U.S. cities.

Technology

Social media, cell phones, and the internet are also transforming the 21st-century political environment. Forty-eight percent of the world is online. By 2020 more people in the world are expected to have mobile phones than to have running water or electricity. Technology is dramatically lowering the cost of collective action, making it easier for like-minded people to find one another and join a common cause, even across vast distances. What's more, social activism is not just for social activists anymore. In a hyperconnected world, bystanders can post cell phone videos that go viral. On April 9, 2017, after United Airlines oversold a flight to Louisville, Kentucky, the airline decided to remove four passengers. One of them, David Dao, refused to deplane. Passengers video-recorded Dao as he was violently dragged from his seat and posted the footage on Twitter and Facebook. Two days later, United's stock had lost $255 million in shareholder value, and analysts began worrying about the ramifications for the airline in the Chinese market, where commenters on social media shared the view that Dao was discriminated against because he was Asian.

The Political Risk Framework

How can companies best manage political risk in this environment? Some hire consultants to provide analysis and advice when they need it. Others rely largely on in-house units. Many employ a hybrid approach. While no one model fits all, we have developed a framework that is broad enough for most companies to apply but suggests specific actions. The framework focuses on four competencies: understanding risks, analyzing risks, mitigating risks that cannot be eliminated, and putting in place a response capability that enables effective crisis management and continuous learning.

At each step in the framework, there are three guiding questions that everyone in any organization can ask to address the most important issues.

Step 1: Understand

What is my organization's political *risk appetite?* Companies, like individuals, approach risk differently. Factors that influence their appetite for it include the time horizon of major investments, the availability of alternative investments, the ease of exiting investments, and visibility to consumers. Companies in extractive industries like oil and gas, for example, undertake long-term investments in distant countries, many of which are governed by autocratic regimes and are prone to social unrest. In addition, these firms' key assets cannot be moved easily. For all those reasons, oil and gas companies must be willing to tolerate substantial political uncertainty. In contrast, consumer-facing industries, such as hotel chains and theme parks, are particularly susceptible to reputational damage and typically have a lower risk appetite as a result.

Is there a shared understanding of our risk appetite? The best companies ensure that political risk is a concern for everyone, from the boardroom to the sales floor. Of course, not everyone in an organization will have a similar take on it: The way lawyers and accountants approach risk differs from the way marketers and product developers do, and those differences need to be sorted through and resolved. At Disney the shared understanding is that "nothing hurts the mouse." Disney essentially sets the political risk appetite close to zero.

In 2006 the Lego Group created a strategic risk management capability, which helped align views on risk across the company. The effort was led by Hans Læssøe, an engineer and a 25-year company veteran who called himself Lego's "professional paranoid." He set up systematic processes for training all new managers about risk; engaging every important business leader, including the board members, in setting the risk appetite; identifying risks; and integrating risk assessment and mitigation into business planning. Læssøe's team even developed a "net earnings at risk" metric that management and the board used to estimate the company's risk exposure annually.

How can we reduce blind spots? Reducing blind spots requires imagination. As one major investor told us, "The biggest mistake is believing the future will look like the present. It almost never does." His firm trains all its associates to ask a simple question, over and over: What if we are wrong? Scenario planning, war-gaming exercises, and other methods can also help firms identify hidden risks. While the tools vary, the goal is the same: fostering creative thinking and guarding against groupthink.

Step 2: Analyze

How can we get good information about the political risks we face? It may sound obvious, but you have to look for good information to find it. Companies sometimes neglect to do this. When General Electric's legendary CEO Jack Welch tried to acquire Honeywell International in 2001, the merger sailed through the U.S. Justice Department review, and Welch assumed that EU approval would soon follow. It didn't. European regulators didn't have the same philosophy about antitrust issues that their American counterparts did; the Europeans focused on the potential impact on competitors, not on consumers. And although European regulators had never rejected a major American merger before, they had come close, nearly scuttling the merger of Boeing and McDonnell Douglas just four years earlier. But Welch and Honeywell's CEO, Michael Bonsignore, were so eager to close the deal that they reportedly never consulted their European antitrust attorneys in Brussels. When it became clear the merger was dead, Welch declared, "You are never too old to get surprised."

How can we ensure rigorous analysis? Richard Feynman, one of the world's great physicists, once said that analysis is how we try not to fool ourselves. Nobody can predict the future, but good risk analysis challenges assumptions and mental models about how it might unfold so that organizations are better prepared.

One useful way to begin is by understanding which assets are most valuable and which are most vulnerable. The more those lists converge, the higher a company's political risk. The backlash against SeaWorld was particularly damaging because trained orcas were so important to the company's brand.

Precisely quantifying vulnerability is impossible. But that doesn't mean managers can't reduce uncertainty. Various tools—from red teams (which assume opposing roles or points of view) to Monte Carlo computer simulations (which project the range and likelihood of outcomes)—can help. The goal is to develop ways of understanding key drivers and possibilities so that surprises aren't so surprising.

FedEx is a model of effective risk management. As the company once said, "[We] may not be able to foresee what will cause the next European truck drivers' strike, but [we] know that ground delays will happen at some point, and when it happens, the backup plans are ready to go." Marriott International has a five-tier color-coded security alert system for all its hotels and continuously assesses whether to move each hotel up or down. The Marriott risk team doesn't know exactly when or where terrorists may strike next. Its system is designed to increase preparedness and safety—by notifying hotel managers about changing conditions that might pose a threat, designating specific tasks for every threat level, and auditing compliance to ensure that everyone knows what to do.

How can we integrate political risk analysis into business decisions? In 2016 a global survey by McKinsey found that only a quarter of executives integrate risk analysis into a formal process. The most popular method for addressing geostrategic risk is to simply do ad hoc analyses as events arise. Lego has a better approach, called "boat spotting"—keeping an eye out for potential risks and opportunities so that you don't "miss the boat." The company has used many risk assessment tools, including analyses of Google Trends search data and scenario planning. But it also understands that more important than the approach is the intention: Simply getting managers to use rigorous political risk analysis—of any variety—to defend investments can significantly improve decision making.

Step 3: Mitigate
How can we reduce exposure to the political risks we have identified? Three strategies are almost always useful: dispersing critical assets (colloquially, don't put all your eggs in one basket), creating surge capacity and slack in the supply chain, and working with others in the industry to share political risk assessments and mitigation strategies. The last approach, which is perhaps the most often overlooked, has been undertaken in the hospitality industry.

In 2005 suicide bombers simultaneously hit Hyatt, Radisson, and Days Inn properties in Amman, Jordan. In the aftermath of the bombings, Marriott's vice president for global safety and security, Alan Orlob, formed a hotel security working group with competitors to share information and best practices—receiving sponsorship from the State Department's Overseas Security Advisory Council.

Do we have a good system and team in place for timely warning and action? Companies that manage political risk well do not sit back waiting for government advisories or quarterly industry reports. To develop better situational awareness, they set up effective warning systems that constantly scan a wide range of sources for information. They also establish protocols so that responses to specific conditions are triggered automatically. These protocols make clear what steps should be taken and by whom. The idea is to reduce decision making on the fly.

Companies on the front lines of managing global political risk often create in-house threat-assessment units staffed with former intelligence and law enforcement professionals who track political developments in real time. Royal Caribbean International's team is led by a 25-year veteran of the FBI. Orlob worked in the U.S. Army Special Forces for 24 years. Chevron's eight-person team of global risk experts has a combined 92 years of experience in government security services. These and other best-practice firms know that dedicating a team to spotting risks and developing a warning system can make all the difference.

How can we limit the damage when something bad happens? Managers can take steps to minimize potential damage long before a crisis unfolds. Relationships with external stakeholders are critical during a crisis, for instance—but building them takes time. Former secretary of state George Shultz often likens good diplomacy to gardening—you have to cultivate relationships with counterparts before you ask them to do something hard on your behalf. The same is true in business.

Step 4: Respond

Are we capitalizing on near misses? All organizations want to learn from failures. Not enough try to learn from events that could have ended poorly but didn't because luck saved the day. Leaders must recognize and correct for the human tendency to ascribe close calls to a system's resiliency when it's just as likely the near miss occurred because of a system's vulnerability. The *Challenger* shuttle tragedy is a classic example: Dangerous erosion of special "O-ring" seals had occurred in shuttle flights before the disaster, but the seals had never completely failed, which led NASA managers to mistakenly believe that failure was not likely.

Are we reacting effectively to crises? Good crisis management can be distilled into five steps: assess the situation, activate a response team, lead with values, tell your story (and be honest!), and do not fan the flames. Crises often involve multiple audiences— consumers, investors, journalists, activists, elected officials, federal regulators, and law enforcement officials, to name a few. Each audience can affect the others, generating new risks and making the situation worse. Managing the dynamics among the interested parties is essential.

Soon after Condi began serving as President George W. Bush's national security adviser, a Chinese fighter jet collided with an American surveillance plane in international airspace. The Chinese pilot was killed, and the U.S. plane had to make an emergency landing in China. Its crew members were detained while the two governments negotiated the terms of their release. For President Bush, the goals were clear: The crew had to be released; America would not apologize for legally conducting surveillance in international airspace; and the relationship with China needed to be maintained. Neither country wanted to escalate the situation, but the negotiations were complicated by multiple audiences. The U.S. government could not just say, "China, you listen only to this part. Congress, you listen only to that part." Condi was on the crisis team that met twice a day to carefully manage the response. That effort included crafting a strategy for communications that would show that the governments were working on the problem but wouldn't increase tensions with each new statement. In the end the crew was released, and the Chinese received a letter from the U.S. ambassador to China, Joseph Prueher, expressing regret for the pilot's death without apologizing for the incident.

Are we developing mechanisms for continuous learning? The best crisis response systems institute feedback loops for learning before disaster strikes, to lower the odds that a crisis will occur and improve the response when one does. Few companies get this right. Indeed, it may surprise you that the best continuous learning organizations that we know of are top-notch football teams. In football errors are everywhere, and success and failure are obvious. Elite coaches study wins as well as losses, analyzing each and every play. They review game tapes, make midgame adjustments, and reshuffle lineups for better matches.

Jim Harbaugh—who coached Stanford's team and the San Francisco 49ers and is now at the University of Michigan—has a track record of turning losing teams into winning ones in just a few seasons. He likes to say, "You are getting better, or you are getting worse. You never stay the same." In the corporate world, mechanisms for continuous learning must involve both the head and the heart: assessments of what to keep doing, what to stop doing, and what to start doing, and an inspirational approach to motivate everyone to join the journey.

Risk Management in Action:
Royal Caribbean's Haitian Crisis

Best-practice companies can attest to the value of understanding potential political risks and getting out ahead of them. Royal Caribbean is a good case in point.

On January 12, 2010, a 7.0-magnitude earthquake struck Haiti, killing an estimated 200,000 people. Three days later a Royal

Five Global Shocks That Rattled Business

PERIODICALLY WE SEE MAJOR EVENTS affect virtually everyone in the global economy. Often these "exogenous shocks" cannot be anticipated. But an organization that has built up its expertise in political risk management can still blunt their impact. Five such shocks have affected the political world—and by extension the business world—since the end of the Cold War.

The most significant was the terrorist attacks of September 11, 2001, which revealed that the United States faced threats from weak and ungoverned areas of the world, not just powerful countries. Ever since the Treaty of Westphalia in 1648 marked the beginning of the modern state system, great powers had been most focused on the dangers posed by other great powers. Not anymore.

The 2008 global financial crisis caused a second shock, leading to greater government intervention in the form of austerity measures and new regulations. It also heightened people's awareness of how the global economy was affecting their personal well-being—and helped give rise to populist backlashes. When you lose your house because of the global financial system, international economics becomes personal.

Third, the Arab Spring and the subsequent unrest across the Middle East increased pressure on both governments and businesses in the region and cast doubt on whether the current state system would endure there. Artificially set at the end of the Ottoman Empire by the French, the British, and the Italians, the national borders of Saudi Arabia, Yemen, Turkey, Iraq, Syria, and the Gulf States cut across regional concentrations of Shia, Sunni, and Kurds. The Syrian civil war has added complexity, displacing nearly 6 million people and

Caribbean cruise ship named *Independence of the Seas* landed in the Haitian port of Labadee, sending 3,000 passengers to swim and bask on a private beach just 85 miles from the hard-hit capital of Port-au-Prince. Public reaction was blistering. The *New York Post's* headline screamed "Ship of Ghouls," and the paper noted that passengers were jet-skiing and sipping rum while Haitians were living nearby in makeshift tents amid squalid conditions.

Royal Caribbean faced a political crisis just as dramatic as the backlash against SeaWorld after the release of *Blackfish*. But for the cruise line, the tide soon turned. Within days prominent news putting an immediate strain on neighboring countries where they've sought shelter. The impact of this refugee crisis on Europe may be long-lasting and fuel a strong sense that the EU no longer protects its borders and citizens from the dangers of the Middle East.

The fourth shock we call "great powers behaving badly." The governments of both China and Russia have become increasingly assertive, reigniting long-running territorial conflicts—over the Ukraine in Russia's case and the East and South China seas in China's.

Finally, nativism, populism, protectionism, and isolationism are making a comeback. Globalization lifted millions of people out of poverty and grew the wealth of millions more. Still, it created losers—people who lacked the skills to compete in the modern economy and those for whom a call center in India, servicing American customers, became a symbol of a threat to them, not an opportunity for a worker in New Delhi. The Brexit vote in 2016 and the election of Donald Trump in the United States—the first time that the country elevated someone with absolutely no government experience to the presidency—stemmed in part from these reactions to globalization. It is telling that in the U.S. election, not one of the candidates—Donald Trump or Bernie Sanders or even the former secretary of state Hillary Clinton—defended free trade.

These five major shocks are straining the international order, affecting power dynamics across countries and the politics within them—with reverberating effects across markets.

organizations ran stories highlighting how Royal Caribbean was in fact docking at the request of the Haitian government and providing desperately needed economic aid. Shortly thereafter, a survey of 4,700 people conducted by the website Cruise Critic found that two-thirds agreed with the company's decision to proceed with scheduled cruises to Labadee.

Royal Caribbean's success in handling the situation went far beyond its well-crafted talking points and midcrisis public relations effort—although those surely helped. The company had begun taking political risk management seriously years before the earthquake. And because it had developed strong competencies for handling man-made political risks in Haiti, it was well positioned to deal with a natural disaster there, too.

The cruise line had begun doing business in Haiti in the 1980s, when the country was wracked by political violence, instability, corruption, and poverty. The first step was finding a location in Labadee that—because of its inaccessibility by road—could provide a secluded and gated haven. Next, Royal Caribbean built ties with residents in the area by, for instance, creating a place for local merchants to sell their goods to disembarked passengers, which generated employment for local villagers. The cruise line also paid per-guest taxes to the government and worked to develop relationships at the national and international levels with Haitian officials, NGOs, think tanks, and UN organizations.

As a result, when the 2010 earthquake struck, the company had a deep reservoir of local understanding, trust, and relationships to draw upon. Its executives consulted with government officials and got their buy-in about continuing previously planned stops at Labadee. The cruise line agreed to contribute $1 million in aid, brought disaster relief supplies in on its ships, donated all Haitian shore-excursion proceeds to earthquake relief, and announced partnerships with high-profile charities to provide additional assistance. When Royal Caribbean was attacked in the press, independent advocates and experts, including NGOs and academics, came to its defense. The Haitian special envoy to the UN offered a quote for a company press release in support of continued dockings on the island.

Just as Royal Caribbean did not suddenly begin managing political risk when the earthquake hit, it did not stop once the immediate press furor died down. Six months after the earthquake, the company announced it was building a new school in Haiti, establishing a strategic partnership with three other companies to provide construction materials for housing and critical infrastructure, and launching a "voluntourism" excursion option for passengers to engage in community service onshore.

The cruise line still faces political risk in Haiti: In 2016 it had to temporarily turn away its ships when the country's presidential election was postponed and antitourism unrest grew. But thanks to effective risk management, Haiti has proved a valuable destination for the cruise line for more than 30 years.

Without good practices in place, Royal Caribbean's reputational crisis could have taken a very different turn. The company understood the political risks it faced in Haiti early on, analyzed them, and instituted a number of mitigation efforts before its first ship ever docked on the country's shores. Finally, Royal Caribbean's response plan was well executed, with clear leadership from the top. Adam Goldstein, the president and chief operating officer of the cruise line, put a human face on the crisis, using his personal blog to post frequent updates about everything from how the company made its decisions to daily meeting notes, responses to media reports, and photos of relief supplies. Company spokespeople stayed on message, expressing their empathy and their commitment to contributing to Haiti's recovery. In the aftermath of the earthquake, all the hard work Royal Caribbean had put into political risk management paid off.

When we started teaching a political risk course several years ago at Stanford, some future trends seemed clear. But in the intervening years, we have both been surprised by political events. We might have predicted that a revanchist Russia would challenge the territorial status quo in Eastern Europe but not that it would annex Crimea. We expected the European Union to face stresses, but we did not expect Brexit. Who would have thought that Donald Trump would be elected president of the United States? Or that in the Philippines, a strongman like Rodrigo Duterte would come to power, turning his country away from the West and toward China?

No one can foresee precisely how history will unfold. But managing political risk doesn't need to be pure guesswork. You do not have to know exactly where the risk will come from to be prepared for it. Just as world-class athletes use training and conditioning to increase their strength, executives, we hope, can use our framework to build up their political-risk-management muscles.

In the end the most effective organizations have three big things in common: They take political risk seriously, they approach it systematically and with humility, and they lead from the top.

Originally published May–June 2018. Reprint R1803L

Note

This article is adapted from *Political Risk: How Businesses and Organizations Can Anticipate Global Insecurity* (Twelve, 2018).

How to Scandal-Proof Your Company

by Paul Healy and George Serafeim

IN THE LATE SUMMER of 2016 allegations that employees of Wells Fargo's retail banking unit had opened more than a million unauthorized accounts and sold customers thousands of unneeded products hit the national news. The scandal cost Wells Fargo dearly. On September 8 the Consumer Financial Protection Bureau (along with the Office of the Comptroller of the Currency and the City and County of Los Angeles) fined the company $185 million—and after revelations of more consumer abuses came out, Wells Fargo would later be fined an additional $1 billion and shell out $575 million to settle legal claims. By the end of September, the bank's stock price had fallen 13%, slashing Wells Fargo's capitalization by some $20 billion, and it continued to stagnate while the market soared. John Stumpf, who resigned as CEO that October, and Carrie Tolstedt, the head of the retail bank who'd announced her retirement that July, were forced by the board to forfeit tens of millions of dollars in pay. Four of the unit's senior managers were terminated for cause. Wells Fargo's reputation was left badly tarnished—a humiliation for the 160-year-old institution.

Misconduct was widespread in the retail unit even though Wells Fargo had control and risk-management systems, which were overseen by its board of directors. So what went wrong? An investigation commissioned by the board found that a warped corporate culture, a decentralized organizational structure, and poor leadership were to blame. The postmortem revealed that much of the illegal behavior had been prompted by pressure to hit overly aggressive sales targets linked to bonuses and promotions. Management had received ample warning signs: From 2000 to 2004 the number of cases in which employees had gamed sales and compensation goals rose 10-fold, and critical articles that raised questions about the new accounts, the pressure on the sales force, and increasing employee turnover had appeared in the *Wall Street Journal* in 2011 and the *Los Angeles Times* in 2013. Yet leaders of the retail bank had blamed a few bad employees for the problems. Accustomed to deferring to the business units, Stumpf simply accepted that explanation.

Unfortunately, the Wells Fargo saga is not unique. White-collar crimes—such as fraud, embezzlement, bribery, and money laundering—have destroyed enormous amounts of shareholder value at companies like Alstom, Odebrecht, Petrobras, Rolls-Royce, Siemens, Telia, Teva Pharmaceutical, VimpelCom, and Volkswagen. In aggregate, the losses add up to billions of dollars. The legal penalties companies incur can be substantial: Siemens was hit with $1.6 billion in fines, Odebrecht $3.5 billion, and Volkswagen about $20 billion. And then there are the business costs: the time and energy that management must devote to cleaning up the mess and negotiating settlements rather than to beating rivals; the reputational damage; the impact on sales, profits, and stock price; declines in employee engagement and productivity; and increases in employee turnover. Research by the University of Washington's Jonathan Karpoff and others indicates that those costs swamp the legal penalties.

In response to high-profile cases and rising public concern, regulators in the United States and other countries have demanded that companies increase their efforts to deter wrongdoing. As a result, almost every multinational company now invests heavily in compliance and espouses zero tolerance of illegal behavior by employees. Yet in practice, increased regulation and controls alone do not guarantee that crimes are detected early or averted. Indeed, both anecdotal evidence and the data indicate that white-collar crime not only is still rampant but is actually rising. In a 2018 PwC survey, 49%

Idea in Brief

The Problem

Despite government-mandated corporate expenditures on systems to deter white-collar crime, data and anecdotal evidence indicate that it's continuing to rise.

The Causes

Extensive research suggests that the real culprit is not the systems but weak leadership and flawed corporate cultures that push employees to make the numbers at all costs.

The Solution

Leaders need to broadcast that crime hurts everyone in the organization, punish perpetrators equally, hire managers with integrity, create decision-making processes that reduce the opportunity for illegal or unethical acts, and champion transparency.

of 7,228 organizations reported that they had experienced economic crime and fraud in the prior year—up from 30% of organizations in a 2009 survey—and that more than half the perpetrators were "internal actors" Meanwhile, stories about white-collar crime—including allegations that Goldman Sachs employees were involved in a multibillion-dollar fraud in Malaysia, that Deutsche Bank helped clients transfer money from criminal activities to tax havens, and that Airbus engaged in corrupt contracting practices—continue to abound in the media.

The root cause of the problem isn't ineffective regulations and compliance systems, however. It's weak leadership and flawed corporate culture.

Indeed, our research reveals that many of the firms hit by major scandals had controls similar to their peers' and, like Wells Fargo, had received early warning signs of impending problems. But at each of those companies, a culture of making the numbers at all costs trumped any concerns about how the targets were being met.

For the past 10 years we've studied white-collar crime and explored how companies can create an environment that discourages it. We used data from individual companies and from surveys by PwC, Transparency International (an NGO founded in 1993 to combat corruption), the World Bank, executive recruiting firms, and other organizations. All told we looked at data on thousands of organizations and individuals. In addition, we interviewed more than 50 senior and middle managers at 10 organizations that had experienced scandals. And in our research we've found time and again that while compliance systems are important, leadership plays a critical role in shaping an organization's attitudes toward preventing crime and its responses when wrongdoing is detected. Yet all too often, executives abdicate responsibility.

In our interviews we heard a common sentiment: Senior executives at most companies that suffered highly publicized transgressions didn't see these incidents as their personal responsibility to address or as evidence that something was fundamentally amiss in their organizations. Rather, those leaders viewed them as extremely rare occurrences caused by "a few bad apples" and insisted that they couldn't have been prevented. Although the leaders accepted the importance of investing in compliance systems and said they expected employees to act with integrity, they typically saw outperforming competitors and wowing investors—not enforcing high legal and ethical standards—as their priorities. Even worse, all too many leaders overlooked questionable business practices or were lenient toward members of their old-boy networks who were caught committing crimes. That indifference trickled down to employees. It encouraged them to develop a "check the box" mentality: to satisfy training and reporting requirements without internalizing the standards that compliance programs are supposed to instill.

Our research also shows that the leaders who *are* effective in combating illicit employee behavior are deeply involved in setting social norms at their firms and in managing the risk of misconduct. They do so by broadcasting a clear message that crime hurts everyone in the organization. They do not make exceptions when they punish perpetrators. They recruit and promote managers who value integrity, and they create decision-making processes that reduce the opportunity for illegal or unethical acts. Finally, they go the extra mile in making their transactions in corrupt countries transparent, are proactive when it comes to cleaning up their industry's dirty practices, and support societal institutions that empower corporate accountability and honest business behavior.

Send the Message That Crime Doesn't Pay

In our work we made two startling discoveries: Business obtained through illicit means adds little or nothing to the bottom line, and people across the company—not just the perpetrators, their supervisors, and the CEO—suffer when a crime is exposed. Leaders need to understand this and spread the word throughout their organizations.

Illegally acquired business isn't very profitable

In public, leaders of multinationals state that their companies do not tolerate corruption. But many turn a blind eye when people in their organizations pay bribes—either directly or through local partners—in developing economies where anticorruption laws are weakly enforced. Their rationale: "We have no choice. If we don't pay bribes, we won't be able to compete in those markets and will suffer financially."

The facts paint quite a different picture. Two cases in point are Siemens and SNC-Lavalin, engineering and construction companies that in the past 12 years were separately charged with bribery. Senior executives at those firms told us that audits conducted afterward revealed that the profits on the transactions involving the illicit payments were unexpectedly low—largely because of the substantial cost of the bribes (as much as 10% of the contract value).

Those companies' experiences appear to be the rule, not the exception. In our research we looked at the financials of 480 multinationals that had been rated by Transparency International in 2006 on the anticorruption systems and activities disclosed in their annual reports and on their websites. When we compared their performance from 2007 through 2010, controlling for industry, host country, stock market listing, and other relevant factors, we found that the firms with poor anticorruption ratings had 5% higher annual sales growth in weakly regulated regions than firms with good ratings did. However, the multinationals with poor ratings also saw *lower profitability* on their sales growth in weakly regulated regions than their highly rated peers did. The profitability differences were comparable in magnitude to the bribes typically paid in those regions.

The extra sales growth generated by illicitly obtained business also doesn't boost shareholder value—even if the bribes go undetected. Using standard valuation models, we found that among poorly rated firms, the increase in shareholder value from additional sales in weakly regulated regions was offset by lower profitability. Of course, if corrupt practices come to light, a company's reputation will suffer and its stock price will take a hit. That is no small risk: When we examined the data from 2007 to 2010, we found that companies with poor anticorruption ratings had a 28% higher likelihood of having a scandal break in the media.

Everyone suffers

Perpetrators of crimes who are punished obviously pay a price financially and professionally. But what is less obvious or widely recognized is the damage to employees who had nothing to do with the crime. When we studied more than 2,000 senior managers (C-level executives and leaders of business units and functions) who had changed employers, we found that people who had left companies with criminal scandals to join new organizations were paid nearly 4% less than their peers. The difference in salaries persisted for years, resulting in a significant loss of wealth for the affected executives—even those who'd left a company *before* a scandal and were completely uninvolved. The cost of this stigma was greater for more-senior executives (a 6.5% difference in annual pay), for women (7%), and in countries with strong regulatory and governance systems (6%).

All these findings, not to mention the legal penalties and business costs, should persuade leaders to take a personal stand against corruption. They should use the data from our and others' research to show people throughout their organizations that crime is costly to the firm and to their own careers, and that it's everyone's job to fight it.

Of course, leaders must also take seriously any concerns raised by employees about possible wrongdoing and performance pressures. A failure to do so makes it more likely that good people will find themselves in situations where they feel compelled to behave badly or to tolerate transgressions. Though that may sound obvious, we have found that in far too many instances, leaders don't act on problems that have been brought to their attention. The board-commissioned postmortem of the Wells Fargo scandal found that Tolstedt, who had led the retail unit since 2007, didn't like to be challenged or to hear negative information; she intimidated people—even senior managers—at the retail bank. Stumpf, the parent bank's CEO, minimized concerns about misconduct in retail banking that were first raised in 2002 and then raised again in 2004 and from 2012 to 2014. When the critical *Los Angeles Times* articles appeared in 2013, Stumpf (and the board) failed to recognize the full harm to customers and adequately investigate the allegations. And although the reports of misconduct under Tolstedt were persistent, Stumpf continued to support her, even when Wells Fargo's lead independent director and the chairman of the board's risk committee suggested that she be dismissed in late 2015.

Ensuring that whistle-blower programs work effectively is crucial. (Recent research conducted by our colleague Eugene Soltes found that 20% of whistle-blower hotlines do not function properly and that organizations with weak internal controls do not permit whistle-blowers to remain anonymous.) Leaders should honor—or at least protect—whistle-blowers, who too often are treated poorly by managers and their colleagues for "ratting out" perpetrators. Even generous financial rewards for whistle-blowing, which can take years to collect, pale in comparison with the steep costs: lost relationships, stress on the individuals and their families, difficulty in landing another job.

Last, leaders must be crystal clear with employees about the behavior they won't tolerate. Interviews we did at Siemens and SNC-Lavalin revealed that those firms' executives failed to set explicit boundaries between acceptable and unacceptable practices for salespeople and business partners operating in highly corrupt countries. One Siemens executive told us that the message employees received from their managers was "Get the business—I do not need to know how you got it."

In contrast, consider the steps a large pharmaceutical maker that had experienced a fraud took to communicate its stance on such behavior: It commissioned Harvard Business School to write a case about the incident and used that case in its own training sessions to help managers diagnose the causes of the problem and brainstorm ways to deter future incidents.

Don't Play Favorites

To make it clear to everyone that they really mean it when they say illicit behavior will not be tolerated, leaders must respond decisively to crimes, dismissing and taking legal action against *all* perpetrators on a uniform basis. Yet anecdotal evidence and our research show that many leaders fail to do this.

Siemens permitted managers caught paying bribes in Italy to retire with full pensions, and it paid a $1.6 million settlement to the departing CFO responsible for overseeing the contract involved. The #MeToo movement's spotlight on harassment and assault faced by women has brought to light numerous cases in which corporate leaders, and in some cases boards, allowed senior male executives to remain in their jobs despite multiple allegations that they had abused female employees. And leaders of the Roman Catholic Church treated clergy accused of child molestation leniently, often by moving them to other parishes rather than expelling them or supporting their prosecution.

To examine whether that kind of permissiveness is pervasive in business, we analyzed the punishments companies gave to perpetrators of white-collar crimes. We used data from a PwC survey that asked firms about their experiences with crime in 2011, including data on the nature of the offenses, punishments, and main-perpetrator demographics. Of the 3,877 firms responding, 608 reported detecting white-collar crimes by employees that year. When we looked at the most serious crime each firm reported, we found that 42% of the main perpetrators had been dismissed or left the organization and faced legal action, 46% had been dismissed with no legal action, and 13% remained with the organization (with or without a transfer or warning). The low rate of legal action against the perpetrators most likely reflects the practical challenges of prosecuting white-collar criminals: Evidence that an individual committed an act doesn't suffice; there also has to be proof that he or she intended to commit it or had knowledge of wrongdoing. Given the potential penalties and reputational risks to companies, corporate attorneys often advise executives to quietly dismiss perpetrators without any legal action.

Treating perpetrators leniently, however, sends a message to potential offenders that crime pays or isn't risky, and it also damages the morale of honest employees. At several companies plagued by crime, the employees we interviewed expressed frustration over their leadership's unwillingness to remove senior managers accused of wrongdoing; the employees said it hurt morale and led some people to quit.

Another troubling finding of our research was the uneven pattern of punishment. Controlling for the type of crime and its magnitude, our analysis of the PwC data revealed that perpetrators who were junior managers or staff members were 24% more likely to face legal action and dismissal than perpetrators who were senior executives. Even when crimes were similar, senior executives were more likely to be given a warning or an internal transfer, and junior managers were more likely to be dismissed.

Undoubtedly, leaders are more reluctant to fire a senior executive because of his or her relationships with customers or the belief that the person's expertise will be difficult to replace. But our findings about how women are treated relative to men suggest that this is not the full story and that cronyism and favoritism are significant factors. Senior women, who are often seen as outsiders in informal male social networks and are less likely to have close personal relationships with the male decision makers who determine punishments, are disciplined more severely than senior men who've committed crimes of the same type and magnitude.

Companies operating in countries with greater workforce gender inequality (such as India, Turkey, Middle Eastern nations, Indonesia, and Italy) were also more likely to impose harsher punishments on senior women than on senior men. In addition, we found that punishments were harsher for senior women at firms that had a weaker commitment to internal controls and that failed to report crimes to regulators, thereby making it easier to respond to them inconsistently.

The obvious remedy is to create and religiously enforce a policy of punishing everyone equally. That's what Erik Osmundsen did at Norsk Gjenvinning (NG), a Norwegian waste management company. Soon after being appointed CEO, in 2012, he set out to eliminate widespread fraud, theft, and corruption at the firm. He created a set of values that included behaving like a responsible entrepreneur—one who did not cut corners—and being a team player within both the company and society. The values were translated into specific codes of conduct for each job, which every employee had to agree to follow. The company then implemented a four-week amnesty period, during which employees could confess any transgressions they had performed or witnessed. After that, nobody was forgiven for any infraction. Altogether about 170 operating and staff managers—roughly half the total—left the firm over the next 18 months. The vast majority chose to quit; a handful were fired. (See "We Were Coming Up Against Everything from Organized Crime to Angry Employees," HBR, July–August 2019.)

Recruit Leaders with a Record of Integrity

To change the culture of a company plagued by systemic crime, you need to bring in new leaders with a reputation for honesty. If the industry itself is rife with corruption, it may be necessary to hire executives from other industries, who will have a different perspective and are likely to shake up the status quo.

Siemens replaced Klaus Kleinfeld, who had stepped down as CEO during the bribery investigation, with Peter Löscher, an executive from the pharmaceutical industry. One key factor in Löscher's appointment, cited in the press release (in a rare move for such announcements), was "his upright character." Recognizing the challenges in changing the culture at Siemens, Löscher brought in from the outside several senior managers whom he had worked with previously and who he knew had high integrity. They included Andreas Pohlmann as chief compliance officer and Peter Solmssen as general counsel and member of the management board. Both men, along with Barbara Kux, who came in as chief sustainability officer and member of the management board, played a critical role in developing a plan to address the problems at the company and reform its culture. (See "The CEO of Siemens on Using a Scandal to Drive Change," HBR, November 2012.)

Since NG's problems were endemic to the waste management industry, Osmundsen opted to recruit fresh blood from outside it (from building materials, aluminum, retail, oil and gas, and soft drink firms). He persuaded people to join NG with his vision of making it a model green company—one that, by pursuing innovative approaches to waste management, could play a significant role in furthering environmental sustainability. In the short term, employee turnover hurt the company's financial performance. But within three years it had recovered financially and was well-positioned for more-profitable growth.

Require Employees to Make Tough Decisions in Groups

When Statoil, a Norwegian energy company (recently renamed Equinor), established a large market presence in Angola, its executives and board recognized that its employees would face pressure to pay bribes there. (Transparency International has ranked Angola one of the most corrupt countries.) To reduce the likelihood that they would succumb, the company's leaders ordered employees to make decisions in groups. This was a direct result of Statoil's experiences in Iran. In 2004 and 2006 the company agreed to pay fines in Norway and the United States, respectively, for bribing a government official to secure a contract in Iran (though the firm neither admitted nor denied guilt). A senior executive told us that one lesson from that scandal was that employees were much more likely to cut corners and do the wrong thing when they made calls on their own.

Making a tough decision in a group requires people to have open and honest discussions, and that doesn't happen automatically. Employees must have faith that other group members are committed to hearing and valuing their opinions and that the firm's leaders will support the group's decisions, even if they have adverse financial consequences. If leaders don't inspire that trust, simply relegating decisions to groups is unlikely to solve the problem. Research by our Harvard colleague Amy Edmondson has shown that it takes strong leadership to create a climate of psychological safety. Leaders must actively promote the behaviors they expect people throughout the organization to adopt—by, for example, showing that it's OK to ask tough questions and express dissenting views, empowering frontline employees to speak frankly to their superiors about signs of potential trouble, being candid about the organization's past errors and openly discussing them, and acknowledging their own ignorance about a topic or area of expertise.

Champion Transparency

After Statoil's bribery charge, Helge Lund, its new CEO at the time, decided that the company would become one of the first firms in an extractive industry to publicly disclose the payments they made to foreign governments to gain access to countries' natural resources—a practice that regulators and public interest groups had long advocated for. This decision sent a strong message to employees that the old ways of conducting business would no longer be tolerated.

Supporting institutions that investigate and report on corruption is another way that leaders can demonstrate to employees that they're serious about conducting business in an ethical fashion. The work of these organizations promotes fair competition and increases the public's confidence that business crimes are detected and punished; and to the extent that it reduces corruption, it stimulates economic development.

Statoil became one of the original members of the Extractive Industries Transparency Initiative (EITI), which aims to bring together companies, governments, and NGOs to reduce corruption in resource-rich countries and increase transparency about payments by oil, gas, and mining companies there. Over time participation in the initiative has steadily increased, and while early EITI reports provided aggregate information on company payments and country revenues, the latest frequently include detailed company disclosures of payments. Collective action appears to be moving things in the right direction: Our empirical research, analyzing data from 186 countries over more than 10 years, suggests that countries with EITI reporting have experienced a significant decrease in corruption, especially those that began with high levels of it.

At Siemens, Löscher and Solmssen reached out to competitors, governments, NGOs, and other stakeholder groups to make a case for broader reform. In 2009, as part of its settlement with the World Bank for its past misconduct, the company agreed to spend $100 million over 15 years to support organizations and projects fighting corruption through collective action, education, and training. By the end of 2017, it had made $73 million in grants for 55 projects. In addition, Siemens became a member of the World Economic Forum's Partnering Against Corruption Initiative (PACI), which includes 87 major companies.

Transparency International and the World Bank (which created a program to fight corruption in 1996) both are active in educating and informing companies and the public. These organizations support research on corruption and regularly rate countries on perceptions of the extent of their public-sector corruption.

Another institution that plays an important role is the media. Smaller organizations that report on corruption are emerging beside the major news outlets. For example, the FCPA Blog publishes news, commentary, and research findings to help compliance professionals, business leaders, and others understand how anticorruption laws work, how corruption arises, and how it affects people and organizations. In Russia, Alexey Navalny operates RosPil, a nonprofit at which a small group of lawyers investigate and report on potential incidents of corruption. In India, Ramesh and Swati Ramanathan have created ipaidabribe.com to provide a platform for people to report incidents when they've been asked to pay a bribe.

Research by Aymo Brunetti of the University of Bern and Beatrice Weder of the Graduate Institute Geneva confirms what you would expect: A free press lowers corruption. But press freedom is under attack: Hostility toward the media is no longer limited to authoritarian countries; it has spread to democratic nations, where efforts to threaten and delegitimize the media are on the rise, according to Reporters Without Borders, an NGO that publishes the annual World Press Freedom Index. Business leaders serious about combating corruption can and should support journalists, by publicly recognizing their legitimacy and defending them when they come under attack.

In large organizations, mistakes will be made. The world is a messy place, and humans are imperfect. But by creating a culture that encourages employees to act ethically and legally, leaders can minimize the likelihood that a scandal will hit their company and increase its ability to bounce back from any illicit actions that do occur. To set the right tone, leaders have to model high standards in both their professional and personal lives.

All too many leaders still fail to continually stress the importance of organizational integrity. They either underinvest in compliance systems or have a check-the-box mentality toward risk management and delegate the responsibility to lawyers and accountants. Red flags go unheeded. When crimes are detected, they're dealt with quietly and unequally. These leaders justify their behavior by saying, "Corruption is an industry problem that we cannot fix," "It's the way business is conducted in these countries," or "We can't afford to lose the business."

In contrast, other leaders, many operating in high-risk countries or sketchy industries, set high standards and practice what they preach. They don't just install strong compliance systems; they also support training programs and performance-feedback and whistleblowing systems; create an atmosphere where it's psychologically safe to speak up when something seems wrong; and engage their industry peers to fight corruption together. Our research indicates that organizations with such leaders don't pay a high financial price for their integrity. Although they may not grow as quickly as their less-scrupulous peers, their growth is more profitable.

Then there are the less widely discussed benefits. Many employees who have chosen to work at high-integrity companies in high-risk countries and industries have told us that they did so because of those firms' values. Some people even told us that they accepted lower pay from those employers. Such companies and their leaders have the respect of their customers, regulators, and communities. They are more likely to prosper and endure.

Where Is Your Company Most Prone to Lapses in Integrity?

by Eugene Soltes

EVERY SIZABLE ORGANIZATION HAS integrity gaps—areas where what's considered appropriate behavior diverges from the norms set by its leaders. Within these pockets, things like offensive language, overly aggressive sales practices, or conflicts of interest may be overlooked or even implicitly condoned. Such lapses not only endanger the reputation of the company but also pose regulatory and liability risks.

Many corporate leaders don't discover the magnitude of integrity gaps until a problem has blown up into a crisis and the threat of government action or litigation looms. Board members are often taken by surprise, asking, Why didn't we spot this earlier? Shouldn't we have known where we were vulnerable and how? Compliance and ethics programs are supposed to prevent such crises, but the people running them are often playing defense rather than strategically rooting out trouble before it grows and spreads. Fortunately, however, company leaders can get ahead of the risks by setting up systems for early detection through routine data collection.

Integrity gaps arise for several reasons. In a geographically dispersed organization, local norms and cultures can vary widely, making it a challenge to set unified standards and expectations. In an extensive global survey examining fraudulent business practices, for instance, EY found that no senior managers in Switzerland approved of misstating financial performance. But the same survey found that more than a quarter of managers in Vietnam and Indonesia were willing to engage in such deception. Attitudes and ethics can also differ by demographic segment. EY's survey revealed that one in five employees under age 35 could justify paying cash bribes to help a business survive an economic downturn, but among employees over 35, only one in eight could.

Before your organization can develop a plan to identify integrity gaps in its culture, it needs to accept two things:

First, *some* misconduct occurs at your firm. When I looked at data from a host of internal reporting sources for three innovative *Fortune* 100 companies—none of which has faced a recent civil or criminal charge—I found that on average, each firm had experienced a violation that could lead to regulatory sanctions (such as a bribe or financial fraud) once every three days. While their organizations have issues more frequently because of their size, these companies also have some of the most robust and effective controls I've seen. Their violations were much smaller than the kind that hit the news, but they illustrate that even companies that invest heavily in compliance will have some malfeasance within their ranks.

Second, a considerable amount of misconduct is not going to be internally reported. Violations that company leaders learn about through traditional channels are probably only the tip of the iceberg—and that should make leaders nervous. Though some attorneys argue that a company shouldn't proactively try to identify misconduct because it could turn into discoverable evidence that might be used against the firm, "ignorance is bliss" is not a sustainable way to run a business. Allowing integrity gaps to grow is especially unwise in an era when employees are increasingly likely to bring allegations straight to the media or regulators if they feel ignored by their leadership.

Gathering Data to Identify Gaps

Once you've acknowledged that integrity gaps exist in your organization, how can you figure out where they are? Just ask.

Randomly giving employees a simple survey can provide a ground-level view of practices that senior leadership may be missing—and help you identify where the problems lie. The survey has three questions:

1. In the past quarter have you observed any of the following? Please check all that apply.

- ☐ Conflicts of interest
- ☐ Sexual harassment
- ☐ Bribes or inappropriate gifts
- ☐ Accounting irregularities
- ☐ Antitrust violations
- ☐ Theft

While the kinds of misconduct companies need to ask about will vary with their business models and risks, the question above includes examples of the most pertinent problem areas. Different organizations, and subgroups within them, will get dramatically varying responses to this part of the survey. I have seen some companies where fewer than 0.5% of employees report observing certain types of questionable behavior. But that figure can reach 10% or more in individual geographic and functional subgroups in some firms.

When analyzing the survey data, you should focus on looking for *integrity* problems rather than strictly *legal* violations. For example, a senior manager might regularly say things that wouldn't legally constitute sexual harassment but that nonetheless make employees deeply uncomfortable. Or an employee might believe he witnessed a payment that would violate the U.S. Foreign Corrupt Practices

Act when it was technically a facilitation payment permitted under the law. These issues are still worth identifying because anything employees perceive to be a violation can affect workplace morale. Moreover, they often can be leading indicators of more-serious misconduct that will develop into legal or regulatory exposure.

2. If you observed questionable conduct, did you report it? Please answer yes or no for each of the following:

Conflicts of interest _____

Sexual harassment _____

Bribes or inappropriate gifts _____

Accounting irregularities _____

Antitrust violations _____

Theft _____

Leaders, especially those who are legally focused, sometimes take false comfort in the fact that they have a code of conduct that requires employees to report any violations they see. In reality, however, that promise is a check-the-box exercise for many employees. The responses to the second question will often illuminate gaps between the code and actual behavior.

Gartner, which is regularly asked to survey companies' employees about their organizational culture, has observed that reporting rates vary significantly for different kinds of violations. Workers are most likely to report a theft of company property or accounting irregularities; 46% of those who observed a theft reported it, and 41% of those who saw fraudulent accounting practices did. However, the reporting rate is considerably lower in other instances, including inappropriate gift giving (27%) and conflicts of interest (34%). Notably, Gartner's data shows that the average reporting rate is less than 50% for all types of violations, whether they're HR related, sales related, or regulatory related.

3. If you noted in question two that you didn't report the questionable conduct, why not?

Conflicts of interest _____

Sexual harassment _____

Bribes or inappropriate gifts _____

Accounting irregularities _____

Antitrust violations _____

Theft _____

The potential reasons employees don't report wrongdoing are numerous. They may fear retaliation, be reluctant to get involved, feel conflicted because the incident involved a friend, or worry that exposing the misbehavior could undermine the firm's goals or financial performance. Fear of retaliation tends to be most common; in surveys done within companies, 10% to 30% of employees list it as their major concern.

Many of the barriers to reporting are institutional problems that require understanding the source of employees' concern. Others, like not wanting to get involved, indicate that the reporting process itself is—or at least is rumored to be—too cumbersome. Companies that work to reduce that perception can increase reporting rates. In a recent internal pilot, compliance leaders at Kimberly-Clark went back to employees who had reported integrity issues (nonanonymously) and asked them whether they felt the reporting process was fair and whether they would recommend it to a colleague. Notably, the compliance executives did not ask whether the people reporting problems agreed with the outcome of investigations; instead they emphasized the aim of improving the process to ensure that people knew their input was valued and respected in the organization. On the basis of the feedback, Kimberly-Clark now is refining how it communicates to and trains people about the reporting process.

To get answers to these three questions, organizations can simply send employees a short "pulse" survey or integrate a survey into routine compliance training. Critically, data collection should be conducted anonymously—that is, without capturing individuals' names or identities—to encourage complete candor. Anonymity can be preserved while the firm gathers nonidentifying metadata, including the location and rank of employees (assuming there are more than a few dozen people in each subgroup). That information will reveal to managers which parts of the organization deserve greater attention. To ensure employee confidentiality, many companies hire a third-party consultant to conduct the surveys and restrict access to their data to in-house compliance, legal, and audit teams.

Learning from the Data

Data from this simple survey can produce three types of insights:

Where to focus

Identifying the location of specific integrity gaps—by both function and geography—can be extremely valuable. By analyzing data on violations in these areas, companies can unearth the causes of misconduct and devise a strategy to address them—perhaps by redesigning incentives, creating new controls, or conducting training.

Identifying gaps is not a onetime HR exercise in finding the "bad apples" and separating them from the good. Violations often happen among the most dedicated and successful employees. These people may even be especially susceptible to certain kinds of misbehavior. For example, high-performing sales employees may feel more pressure to inappropriately book sales if they're behind on the budget at the end of a quarter. This is why data collection should be done periodically across different groups of employees throughout the year. Ideally, each quarter a randomized subset of employees would be surveyed.

Better ways for employees to voice concerns

While it may be obvious that norms will differ among countries, offices, and even teams, figuring out how they differ and what to do about them is a challenge. Employees' survey responses helped a large consumer products company tackle this. From them the firm learned that in one country where citizens feared monitoring and reprisal by an authoritarian government, workers were hesitant to call their local integrity hotline. To make them more comfortable about reporting their concerns, the company created a toll-free number for them in the United Kingdom.

The true size of the iceberg

To prevent wrongdoing, you need to understand issues that may be developing below the surface. Yet it's often difficult to know what kinds of problems are slipping through compliance processes (like hotlines) and other internal controls. The survey data can help companies better estimate the actual amount of misconduct within the organization—and the amount that's not being reported. Ultimately, this kind of modeling will help senior leaders get a clearer picture of the integrity issues and violations that otherwise would probably never come to their attention.

Many leaders publicize their firms' commitment to integrity and say that their employees should feel empowered to speak up if they see something questionable. Yet the best leaders don't rely on these statements alone. Instead they collect data to monitor and assess whether their organizations actually adhere to their ethical standards. Sustaining a company's cultural integrity requires constant vigilance—and measuring progress is the best way to manage it effectively. Data that allows leaders to proactively identify emerging gaps is a critical tool for staying one step ahead of problems that might land their companies in the next day's headlines.

Originally published July–August 2019. Reprint R1904B

Beating the Odds When You Launch a New Venture

by Clark G. Gilbert and Matthew J. Eyring

FOR NEARLY 20 YEARS the case study used to introduce Harvard Business School's Entrepreneurial Management course has been Howard Stevenson's "R&R." It looks at Bob Reiss, an entrepreneur who launches a venture in the board-game industry. Students are encouraged to explore all the production, development, distribution, and marketing costs associated with the new venture.

A cursory reading of the case suggests that it's a lesson in the rewards that come to an entrepreneur who is willing to take on an enormous amount of risk. Reiss capitalizes on what he correctly foresees is an ephemeral opportunity to ride the coattails of the Trivial Pursuit craze before me-too products flood the market. But a more careful analysis reveals something else entirely. At every turn, Reiss seeks to reduce his risks before making any significant financial investments or operational commitments. For example, he pre-sells a sizable number of units to ensure cash flow. As students come to understand, Reiss actually limits his at-risk capital to the cost of the game design and the prototype. Rather than the high-risk, high-reward seeker he initially seems, Reiss proves to be a manager who constantly identifies risks and finds creative ways to remove them.

Over the past decade we have participated in the development of a dozen or so corporate ventures and served on new-venture boards at a host of companies, including Johnson & Johnson, the Scripps Media Center, and Landmark Media Enterprises. Although many of the ideas in this article come from our direct work with new ventures, they also reflect more than 10 years of collaborative thinking by the Entrepreneurial Management teaching group at HBS.

What has become clear to us is that the most effective corporate innovators are the ones who follow the same discipline Bob Reiss did. Success comes to those who quickly identify and systematically eliminate risks in the right order, using the right level of resources and the right methods.

Recognize That Not All Risks Are Created Equal

New ventures fairly bristle with risks. If managers attempted to eliminate all of them, the products or services would never get to market. The key question is "What's the most important uncertainty?" and the answer should be targeted early. In considering how to answer that question, we have found it useful to think in three broad, sometimes overlapping categories: deal-killer risks, path-dependent risks, and easy-win, high-ROI risks.

Deal-killer risks

As the name implies, these are uncertainties that, if left unresolved, could undermine the entire venture. Such risks may be less obvious in the moment than they appear in hindsight, after catastrophe has struck. That's because they often take the form of unwarranted or unexamined assumptions about the premises underpinning the venture. For example, a colleague of ours was an early employee at a startup satellite radio company aimed at consumers in the developing world. The premise of the venture was that satellite broadcasting technology would be a relatively cost-effective way to bring mass media to markets that lacked infrastructure. Market research suggested that a huge latent need would turn into a booming business. The company deftly negotiated broadcasting licenses in several

Idea in Brief

Despite stereotypes to the contrary, the best entrepreneurs are relentless about managing risks—indeed, that's their core competency. As the risk level of a new venture goes down, the value goes up.

Risks should be uncovered and hedged in order of their importance and affordability: deal-killers first; then the risk of settling too

early on a strategic direction; and finally, operational risks that can be disposed of quickly and cheaply.

All new ventures are partly wrong and partly right. Run small, cheap, fast experiments to determine which bits are which and what course corrections you need to make.

developing countries and solved a number of complex technological challenges. Nevertheless, the business imploded. What was the problem?

As it turned out, the demand identified by market research depended on customers' being able to access the broadcasts through low-cost radio receivers—which turned out to be impossible. The radio receiver required complex features such as multimode playback, a keypad for ordering subscription services, and—worst of all—professional installation, which made the device unaffordable in most of the developing world. Having failed to identify this fatal vulnerability, the company invested hundreds of millions of dollars to reach consumers who couldn't pay for its service. The business limped along before ultimately going bankrupt. The company should not have left this key deal-killer assumption so utterly untested until late in the life of the venture. Quick-hit market research and rapid prototyping could have provided early warning signals.

Path-dependent risks

Rare is the new venture that never has to confront strategic forks in the road to success. Path-dependent risks arise when pursuing the wrong path would involve wasting large sums of money or time or both. For example, consider the question confronting E Ink, a supplier of electronic paper display technologies in Cambridge, Massachusetts.

Tackling the Right Risks First

RISK AND VALUE ARE INVERSELY PROPORTIONAL: When you remove risk, you increase value. But it matters in what sequence you tackle risks, because not all of them are created equal.

Suppose a manager is launching a new e-commerce business. He must remove a number of risks before the venture reaches its peak value. He could simply remove them as they occur to him.

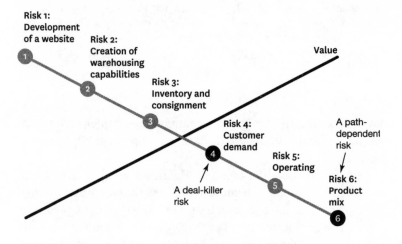

In the company's early days there was great debate over whether its electronic "ink" would best be used for large-area display signage, flat-panel screens for ebooks, or the more ambitious radio-paper products, which could be programmed and updated remotely. Each option had different technical, marketing, and distribution requirements; if the company chose wrong, it risked misallocating millions of dollars.

Rather than choosing one path and hoping for the best, E Ink reduced the cost of pursuing all three by outsourcing its marketing and production capabilities and then focused on resolving the risks associated with the core technology for all three applications. Thus, when display signage proved less successful, the company was not locked into a single market, and the technical knowledge it had developed allowed the fledgling venture to successfully license its technology for more viable products—most notably Amazon's Kindle.

But unless he confirms demand, it doesn't matter how provocative his website is; customers won't buy. And if he doesn't answer the product-mix question, he will fill his warehouse with products he can't sell.

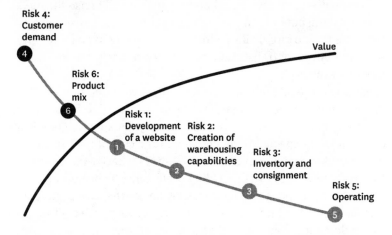

Addressing these two risks early creates disproportionate value quickly, not only saving critical resources but also moving the venture in the right direction sooner.

Risks that can be resolved without spending a lot of time and money

Even after entrepreneurs have considered both deal-killer and path-dependent risks, many uncertainties will remain on the table. If every one were addressed, they'd never get their products to market. But the more risks that can be eliminated, and the faster they can be removed, the greater the odds of success. Accordingly, successful entrepreneurs also look for risks that are quick and cheap to resolve, applying a cost-benefit approach that we think of as the "experimental ROI"—the amount of risk that can be reduced for each dollar invested in an experiment designed to resolve it. For example, one of the earliest experiments that Reed Hastings, the founder of Netflix, conducted in developing his movie-rental-by-mail business was to mail himself a CD in an envelope. By the time it arrived undamaged,

133

he had spent 24 hours and the cost of postage to test one of the venture's key operational risks.

Fail to spot a deal-killer risk, and your venture is doomed. Fail to hedge a path-dependent risk, and you dramatically raise the odds that you'll run out of funds before you ever come to market—or will get there far too late. Fail to address a high-ROI risk in an orderly way, and you may transform a temporary setback into an insurmountable obstacle.

Such was the fate of a startup we worked with that targeted the nascent medical tourism market. The venture's value proposition was to fly patients overseas for high-quality, inexpensive medical care, which it expected to deliver at half the cost of the same care in the United States. Several deal-killer risks faced the venture. Unfortunately, rather than tackling them early, by beginning with those that could be tested most quickly and at the least cost, team members plunged into a time-consuming and expensive effort. To gauge demand, they conducted a series of long interviews with *Fortune* 500 corporate benefits managers and insurers around the country. Things looked very promising. However, not until they'd put in nearly six months of work and spent considerable money on travel did they decide to do something they should have done early on: run two simple, high-ROI experiments to test key risks. The first involved a seminar to introduce the concept to prospective patients. The second involved several phone calls to U.S. hospitals to discover their unpublished discount prices for certain procedures. In only two weeks (and at virtually no expense), the team learned that patient demand was actually quite tepid and limited to a very narrow band of procedures, and that U.S. hospitals were willing to lower their prices—to near international levels in some cases—if patients paid cash up front. By failing to address their greatest risk—that no market existed for their services—in the cheapest and fastest way, the team members wasted significant resources and missed a critical opportunity to redirect their strategy to something more promising, such as a venture restricted to regional medical travel within the U.S or travel to a close international destination like Mexico.

A common mistake is to focus on one key risk to the exclusion of others. Sometimes you must be satisfied with partial risk resolution in one area, even as you start to consider and work on risk in another. As a general rule, we have found it's best to select a "stake in the ground" customer early in the life of the venture. You can then confirm a rough price point at which customers can be served, even as you continue to reduce related technical risk.

Be Judicious with Capital

All other things being equal, a large corporation's deep pockets should give it an advantage over bootstrap entrepreneurs when it comes to financing a new venture. But in practice, a parent company's funding procedures are often a major liability—something one of our colleagues, Brad Gambill, has referred to as "the curse of too much capital." Corporations typically allocate money for a new venture all at once, hoping for a large payoff fairly soon. The more money that is sunk into a project at the outset, the less patience the company tends to have and the more people believe in the validity of their original approach, even in the face of evidence to the contrary.

The way venture capitalists invest in startups—by providing capital in multiple rounds as the value of the venture increases—is far more effective. As one of our colleagues puts it, "With each risk you pull off the table, value goes up proportionally." The lower the risk, the greater the value, so this approach favors entrepreneurs who use early funding to reduce the greatest risks—allocating sufficient funds to test the deal-killer risks first and the path-dependent risks as quickly as possible, and then squeezing the most value out of their scarce resources by systematically working through the remaining risks according to the principle of "spend a little to learn a lot."

At many big companies, a project's status correlates almost perfectly with the amount of money invested in it. The competitive advantage of autonomous startups is that they have too little money to go far in the wrong direction.

We can demonstrate the power of this dynamic with two very different examples. Vermeer Technologies, a startup based in Cambridge,

Massachusetts, had only one product: a website development tool called FrontPage. The company was eventually sold to Microsoft, and Microsoft FrontPage became the most widely used web-design software package in the world. But that's not where Vermeer's strategy began. In the early 1990s its founders had hoped to create an interface that would allow users to access content through a common reader across a wide network of computers all over the world. There was only one problem: A nascent service—the World Wide Web—was free to anyone who wanted to access it. After Vermeer's founders learned more about the Web, they decided to take another path altogether, devising a software tool that let nontechnical programmers create their own websites. Reflecting on their original strategy, the founders laugh in relief that they didn't make any significant investment at the outset, because they might have poured their capital into building an ultimately worthless company.

An equally instructive example with a less fortunate outcome is that of Joint Juice, a Bay Area company founded by an orthopedic surgeon who came up with the breakthrough idea of converting glucosamine, effective in reducing joint pain, from a large pill into a more convenient liquid. A strong conviction that his target market was young to middle-aged athletes led to a series of expensive choices relating to the product's caloric load, packaging, distribution channel, and marketing approach. Lavish advertising campaigns were built around professional and Olympic athletes. These early, high-cost investments became self-reinforcing.

Just as data were beginning to reveal that the real demand lay with an older demographic—people who wanted lower-calorie, less-expensive products—an opportunity arose to go national with two large grocery chains. Sunk costs made the opportunity more tempting than it should have been, and Joint Juice signed an expansion contract replete with the high slotting fees associated with grocery retail. When it became clear that the channel and market were wrong, the enterprise was already locked in to a product incorrectly formulated, positioned, and distributed. Today Joint Juice has been adapted to the right market, but only after millions of dollars more were invested—and significant changes were made to the management team.

Test Early, Test Cheaply

PERHAPS THE MOST DANGEROUS RESULT of injecting too much money too soon into a venture is that it creates a confirmation bias in the minds of venture managers. Instead of testing their assumptions, they become more and more invested in confirming them. But successful entrepreneurs do the opposite: They devise low-cost experiments to disprove a concept before it's too late.

We've found two types of experiments helpful in our work.

Targeted Experiments

These are designed to pinpoint a deal-killer or path-dependent risk. Examples might include running tests on battery life before launching a new portable device, checking for toxicity in a drug before running full-scale efficacy tests, and testing bandwidth and connectivity concerns before launching an online learning program at various locations across the country.

Integrated Experiments

These are designed to test how various elements—the actual business model and operations—work together. In essence, they involve launching the business, or some part of it, in miniature. Although pilot programs are nothing new, our experience suggests that entrepreneurs rarely give them sufficient time to play out. An exception is Aaron Kennedy, who founded Noodles & Company, a chain of quick-casual restaurants. From the beginning Kennedy intended to take his concept nationwide, but he started with just three restaurants. He revised the menu, varied the décor and tested several pricing structures. For almost an entire year he focused on sharpening the concept and making it work on a small scale. Today the chain has more than 218 locations in 18 states.

An integrated experiment may be a pilot, a test-site location, a prototype, or any other trial operation. It might include tests to "launch" the business in a way that allows customers to purchase the product in a real transactional environment. Targeted experiments such as surveys and focus groups can provide insights, but those that come from placing the product in a sales channel where customers make actual purchase decisions are often much deeper.

We cannot make this point too strongly: At the start of a new venture, the only thing you can know about your initial strategy is that it's probably part right and part wrong. One of our colleagues conducted a study of the *Inc.* 500 entrepreneurs and found that most successful ventures had redirected their strategy at least five times before they hit a solid growth trajectory. If you go full speed in your first direction, you'll compromise your ability to figure out which part is wrong—and pay a high price when you eventually do figure it out. But if you invest in stages, spending small sums on the assumption that your strategy will need adjustment, you'll find it much easier to adapt quickly and reach a winning outcome.

Manage Experiments Efficiently

Identifying and prioritizing risks correctly and then conceiving and funding experiments to resolve them systematically will make the unpredictable process of launching a new venture as efficient as it can be. You can take several steps to make your experiments more effective.

Limit the duration
According to Meg Whitman, the former president and CEO of eBay, the company succeeded in its earliest days by recognizing that perfection is sometimes the enemy of the good. It's often better to get something into the market quickly, learn from it, and move on to the next phase of development than to analyze an idea to death and try to perfect it before launch. Even deal-killer risks can sometimes be tested quickly and simply. For example, Innosight Ventures saw an opportunity to serve consumers in India who couldn't afford washing machines but wanted an alternative to the traditional *dhobi* services, which are slow, use dirty water and inferior detergents, and beat clothes on rocks to remove the water from them. The venture managers needed only 60 days to move from completion of the business plan to an initial market test. The test was simple but powerful: They invested a few thousand dollars to build a kiosk that contained a washing machine and a dryer and put it on a busy street corner to see if people were willing to pay 40 rupees (about $1) per kilogram to wash their clothes. It was essentially a mini-launch designed to answer the key question in their business plan: Is there unmet demand for an inexpensive laundry service? Several weeks of growing customer demand at the site indicated a high likelihood that the concept and pricing were essentially sound and with further refine-

ment could exceed estimated break-even levels. Today more than two dozen kiosks have been set up in several Indian cities, and there are plans to expand the business to more than a thousand over the next few years.

Test one thing at a time

Poorly designed experiments vary too many factors at once, increasing the expense and making it difficult to determine what causes what. Experiments should be simple and focused on resolving uncertainties one by one. At a large media company we worked with, the venture managers ran experiments to test a new website registration system that would allow them to target various demographic segments with ads. They didn't know whether registration should be required or optional. Accordingly, their experiment was designed to answer the questions Will people be discouraged from visiting the sites if they are forced to register? and Will people register at all if they aren't required to? Instead of running tests over an entire network of websites, they picked two comparable sites and for a month ran one with an opt-in registration and the other with a forced registration. Everything else was held constant—promotion, launch, investment, and so forth. When the forced registration didn't reduce site visits significantly, they had their answer.

Apply the lessons learned

Too often managers miss the whole point of these experiments. They are meant to help redirect a venture, not to confirm that your initial ideas were correct. Some of our colleagues call this discovery-driven learning. Recall the data on the *Inc.* 500 ventures—five major course corrections for every successful venture. Sometimes those corrections come painfully, but it's better to choose to adjust early than be forced to adjust later.

Be willing to turn off experiments

This idea is closely related to the previous point, but requires far more discipline. Some ventures are simply not going to work. A deal-killer risk may in fact kill the deal. The sooner you cut your losses in such

Case Study

ROBIN WOLANER, WHO LAUNCHED *Parenting* magazine, began with an insight: Large numbers of highly educated women were having children much later in their professional careers than had been true in the past. She raised a small amount of seed capital to push her idea for a magazine forward and chose to spend it on answering the one question that, if unresolved, would render all other risks moot: Is there a differentiated need and a real demand for this product?

Wolaner sent out direct-response cards describing a magazine that would focus on both parents and would have a uniquely sophisticated editorial orientation. Early market tests typically get a response rate of 3% to 4%. Her cards came back at greater than 7%. Because this deal-killer risk was pulled off the table at the outset, valuation jumped from less than $500,000 to more than $5 million.

cases, the sooner you can go on to the next venture. More often, though, the principle applies to some specific component of the venture. We've watched executives in the newspaper industry struggle with this as they've tried to migrate from print media to digital content. One senior manager confessed to us, "We had a thousand experiments running; some of them were working and some of them were not. Sometimes the challenge isn't turning them on—it's turning them off." When an entrepreneur learns that a product or an approach won't work, it is critical to end the experiment and move in a new direction.

New venture formation will always be fraught with risks. We don't want to imply that a systematic approach to identifying and mitigating them will eliminate them. But we do take issue with the notion that it's the risks that produce the rewards. As Bob Reiss's story has illustrated for decades—and our experience continues to confirm—great entrepreneurs don't take risks; they manage them. Quickly determining what's right and what's wrong with key assumptions and then making speedy adjustments often means the difference between failure and success. As entrepreneurial managers learn to do this, they bend the risk-reward curve in their favor and beat the odds.

Originally published May 2010. Reprint R1005G

The Danger
from Within

by David M. Upton and Sadie Creese

WE ALL KNOW ABOUT the 2013 cyberattack on Target, in which criminals stole the payment card numbers of some 40 million customers and the personal data of roughly 70 million. This tarnished the company's reputation, caused its profits to plunge, and cost its CEO and CIO their jobs. What's less well known is that although the thieves were outsiders, they gained entry to the retail chain's systems by using the credentials of an insider: one of the company's refrigeration vendors.

Target's misfortune is just one recent example of a growing phenomenon. External attacks—pervasive intellectual-property hacking from China, the Stuxnet virus, the escapades of Eastern European gangsters—get plenty of attention. But attacks involving connected companies or direct employees pose a more pernicious threat. Insiders can do much more serious harm than external hackers can, because they have much easier access to systems and a much greater window of opportunity. The damage they cause may include suspension of operations, loss of intellectual property, reputational harm, plummeting investor and customer confidence, and leaks of sensitive information to third parties, including the media. According to various estimates, at least 80 million insider attacks occur in the United States each year. But the number may be much higher, because they often go unreported. Clearly, their impact now totals in the tens of billions of dollars a year.

Many organizations admit that they still don't have adequate safeguards to detect or prevent attacks involving insiders. One reason is that they are still in denial about the magnitude of the threat.

Over the past two years we have been leading an international research project whose goal is to significantly improve the ability of organizations to uncover and neutralize threats from insiders. Sponsored by the Centre for the Protection of National Infrastructure (CPNI), which is part of the United Kingdom's MI5 security service, our 16-member team combines computer security specialists, business school academics working on corporate governance, management educators, information visualization experts, psychologists, and criminologists from Oxford, the University of Leicester, and Cardiff University.

Our cross-disciplinary approach has led to findings that challenge conventional views and practices (see the sidebar "Common Practices That Don't Work"). For example, many companies now try to prevent employees from using work computers to access websites not directly connected with their jobs, such as Facebook, dating sites, and political sites. We think they should instead give employees the freedom to go where they want on the web but use readily available security software to monitor their activities, thus yielding important information about behaviors and personalities that will help detect danger. In this article we share our findings on effective ways to minimize the likelihood of insider attacks.

An Unappreciated Risk

Insider threats come from people who exploit legitimate access to an organization's cyberassets for unauthorized and malicious purposes or who unwittingly create vulnerabilities. They may be direct employees (from cleaners up to the C-suite), contractors, or third-party suppliers of data and computing services. (Edward Snowden, who famously stole sensitive information from the U.S. National Security Agency, worked for an NSA contractor.) With this legitimate

Idea in Brief

The Threat

Cyberattacks involving insiders—employees, suppliers, or other companies legitimately connected to a company's computer systems—are pernicious and on the rise. They account for more than 20% of all cyberattacks. Widely used safeguards are ineffective against them.

The Key

To reduce their vulnerability to insider attacks, companies should apply the same approach they used to improve quality and safety: Make it part of everyone's job.

The Solution

Employees should be monitored rigorously and told what threats are likely so that they can report suspicious activities. Suppliers and distributors should be required to minimize risks and should be regularly audited. Leaders should work closely with their IT departments to ensure that crucial assets are protected.

access they can steal, disrupt, or corrupt computer systems and data without detection by ordinary perimeter-based security solutions—controls that focus on points of entry rather than what or who is already inside.

According to Vormetric, a leading computer security company, 54% of managers at large and midsize organizations say that detecting and preventing insider attacks is harder today than it was in 2011. What's more, such attacks are increasing both in number and as a percentage of all cyberattacks reported: A study by KPMG found that they had risen from 4% in 2007 to 20% in 2010. Our research suggests that the percentage has continued to grow. In addition, external attacks may involve the knowing or unknowing assistance of insiders. The Target incident is a case in point.

Causes of Growth

A number of factors in the changing IT landscape explain this rising threat. They aren't particularly surprising—and that's just the point. The doors that leave organizations vulnerable to insider attacks are mundane and ubiquitous.

A dramatic increase in the size and complexity of IT

Do you know which individuals are managing your cloud-based services, with whom you cohabit in those servers, and how safe the servers are? How trustworthy are those who provide you with other outsourced activities, such as call centers, logistics, cleaning, HR, and customer relationship management? In 2005 four Citibank account holders in New York were defrauded of nearly $350,000 by call center staffers based in Pune, India. The culprits were employees of a software and services company to which Citibank had outsourced work. They had collected customers' personal data, PINs, and account numbers.

"Dark Web" sites, where unscrupulous middlemen peddle large amounts of sensitive information, now abound. Everything from customers' passwords and credit card information to intellectual property is sold on these clandestine sites. Insiders are often willing to provide access to those assets in return for sums vastly less than their street value, contributing to the "cybercrime-as-a-service" industry.

Employees who use personal devices for work

Increasingly, insiders—often unwittingly—expose their employers to threats by doing work on electronic gadgets. Our team and others have found that companies' security groups cannot keep up with the dangers posed by the explosion of these devices. According to a recent Alcatel-Lucent report, some 11.6 million mobile devices worldwide are infected at any time, and mobile malware infections increased by 20% in 2013.

It's not just smartphones and tablets that are to blame: The devices can be as simple as flash drives or phone memory cards. "The best way to get into an unprepared company is to sprinkle infected USB sticks with the company's logo around the car park," says Michael Goldsmith, a member of our team and an associate director of Oxford's Cyber Security Centre, referring to the 2012 attack on DSM, a Dutch chemical company. "Some employee is bound to try one of them."

It was widely reported that delegates attending a G20 summit near Saint Petersburg in 2013 were given USB storage devices and

Managers in the Dark

WE ASKED 80 SENIOR MANAGERS about their awareness of insider cyber-security threats and followed up with in-depth case studies of actual incidents. Here's a summary of what we found:

- Managers across all countries and most industries (banks and energy firms are the exception) are largely ignorant of insider threats.

- They tend to view security as somebody else's job—usually the IT department's.

- Few managers recognize the importance of observing unusual employee behavior—such as visiting extremist websites or starting to work at odd times of the day—to obtain advance warning of an attack.

- Nearly two-thirds of internal and external security professionals find it difficult to persuade boards of directors of the risks entailed in neglecting the insider-threat issue.

- Few IT groups are given guidance regarding which information assets are most critical, what level of risk is acceptable, or how much should be invested to prevent attacks.

---

mobile phone chargers laden with malware designed to help steal information. And the Stuxnet computer worm that sabotaged Iran's uranium-refinement facility in 2008–2010 was reportedly introduced via USB flash drives into systems not connected to the internet.

In truth, we are all vulnerable.

The explosion in social media

Social media allow all sorts of information to leak from a company and spread worldwide, often without the company's knowledge. They also provide opportunities to recruit insiders and use them to access corporate assets. The so-called romance scam, in which an employee is coaxed or tricked into sharing sensitive data by a sophisticated conman posing as a suitor on a dating website, has proved to be particularly effective. Other strategies include using knowledge gained through social networks to pressure employees: A cyberblackmailer may threaten to delete computer files or install pornographic images on a victim's office PC unless the sensitive information is delivered.

Why They Do It

A number of government and private case studies have established that insiders who knowingly participate in cyberattacks have a broad range of motivations: financial gain, revenge, desire for recognition and power, response to blackmail, loyalty to others in the organization, and political beliefs.

One example we heard about during our research was a 2014 attack by a spurned suitor on a small but growing virtual-training company. A manager there had complained to his superior about the person in question—a systems administrator who had been sending him flowers at work and inappropriate text messages and had continually driven past his home. Once clearly rejected, the attacker corrupted the company's database of training videos and rendered the backups inaccessible. The company fired him. But knowing that it lacked proof of his culpability, he blackmailed it for several thousand euros by threatening to publicize its lack of security, which might have damaged an upcoming IPO. This costly incident—like most other insider crimes—went unreported.

Insider collaboration with organized crime and activist groups is becoming increasingly common. Many countries are now operating computer emergency readiness teams (CERTs) to protect themselves against this and other types of attack. Of the 150 cases that were analyzed by the CERT Insider Threat Center at Carnegie Mellon University for its 2012 report *Spotlight On: Malicious Insiders and Organized Crime Activity,* 16% had links to organized crime.

One case was the 2012 theft by a Russian gang of details of 3.8 million unencrypted bank accounts and almost 4 million tax returns from the South Carolina Department of Revenue. Forensics showed that the attack was facilitated by an employee who clicked on a link in an email, enabling the gang to steal the employee's credentials and access the state's data servers.

Monica Whitty, a psychologist at the University of Leicester and a member of our team, and many others say that insiders who willingly assist or engage in cyberattacks suffer from one or more conditions in the "dark triad": Machiavellianism, narcissism, and psychopathy. Supporting this view, a 2013 study by CPNI found that inside attackers typically have some combination of these personality traits: immaturity, low self-esteem, amorality or lack of ethics, superficiality, a tendency to fantasize, restlessness and impulsiveness, lack of conscientiousness, manipulativeness, and instability.

Roger Duronio, a UBS Wealth Management systems administrator convicted of using a malicious "logic bomb" to damage the company's computer network in 2006, exhibited a number of these traits. Duronio was worried about the security of his job and became livid when he received only $32,000 of the $50,000 bonus he had expected. So he shorted the company's stock and set off the bomb. It took down as many as 2,000 servers in UBS offices around the United States; some of them couldn't make trades for several weeks. The company suffered $3.1 million in direct costs and millions of dollars more in undisclosed incidental losses. Duronio was sentenced to 97 months in prison for the crime.

How to Think about the Problem

Managing insider cybersecurity threats is akin to managing quality and safety. All were once the responsibility of one specialty department. But organizations can no longer anticipate every risk, because the technology environment is so complex and ever changing. Thus the leaders of enterprises large and small need everyone in the organization to be involved. Here are five steps they should take immediately:

Adopt a robust insider policy
This should address what people must do or not do to deter insiders who introduce risk through carelessness, negligence, or mistakes. The policy must be concise and easy for everyone—not just security and technology specialists—to understand, access, and adhere to. The rules must apply to all levels of the organization, including senior management. A framework provided by the State of Illinois is one model. Here's a link to it: www.illinois.gov/ready/SiteCollec tionDocuments/ Cyber_SOSSamplePolicy.pdf.

Common Practices That Don't Work

THE MOST COMMON cybersecurity safeguards are much less effective against insiders than against outsiders.

Access Controls

Rules that prohibit people from using corporate devices for personal tasks will not keep them from stealing assets.

Vulnerability Management

Security patches and virus checkers will not prevent or detect access by malevolent authorized employees or third parties using stolen credentials.

Strong Boundary Protection

Putting critical assets inside a hardened perimeter will not prevent theft by those authorized to access the protected systems.

Password Policy

Mandating complex or frequently changed passwords means that they often end up on Post-it notes—easy pickings for someone with physical access.

Awareness Programs

Simply requiring employees to read the company's IT security policy annually will not magically confer cyberawareness on them. Nor will it prevent staff members from taking harmful actions.

Employees should be given tools that help them adhere to the policy. For example, systems can be designed to flash a warning message on the screen when someone attempts to log into a subsystem that holds sensitive materials. The system could ask whether the person is authorized to be there and record and track those who are not.

Policy violations should incur penalties. Obviously, an employee who commits a serious offense such as selling customers' personal data or knowingly inserting malware in company systems should be fired and prosecuted. A first offense for something less serious, such as sharing passwords to enable trusted colleagues to access corporate systems, might result in a warning that goes into the employee's record.

What Can *You* Do?

SOME OF THE MOST important activities that nontech leaders should ask of their IT departments are:

- monitoring all traffic leaving enterprise networks via the internet or portable media, and promptly reporting anything unusual or in violation of policy

- staying current with best practices for supporting cybersecurity strategy and policy

- rigorously implementing network defense procedures and protocols that take into account the operational priorities of the business

- actively updating user accounts to ensure that employees never have more access to sensitive computer systems than is absolutely necessary

- making frequent threat assessments and briefing the company's leadership on them

You should also help employees understand how to safely conduct day-to-day tasks. Policy should be regularly reinforced with information sessions and internal communications campaigns, which might include posters in the workplace. Some companies screen videos demonstrating how policy violations can enable cyberattacks and how safer practices might have prevented them.

Raise awareness
Be open about likely threats so that people can detect them and be on guard against anyone who tries to get their assistance in an attack. Customize training to take into account what kinds of attacks workers in a particular operation might encounter. Phishing is a common way to gain entry: Phony emails trick employees into sharing personal details or access codes or into clicking on a link that downloads malware. (Many people don't realize that the "from" address in an email is easy to forge.) It is possible to test your staff's vulnerability to such attacks—either on your own or by employing an external security service.

Even so, it can be difficult to defend insiders against a determined outsider. In April 2013 a French multinational company was the object of a clever attack. One vice president's administrative assistant received an email that referenced an invoice on a cloud-based file-sharing service. She had the sense not to open the file, but minutes later she received a phone call from someone who convincingly claimed to be another vice president at the company and instructed her to download and process the invoice. She complied. The invoice contained a remote-access Trojan that enabled a criminal enterprise apparently based in Ukraine to take control of her PC, log her keystrokes, and steal the company's intellectual property.

Encourage employees to report unusual or prohibited technologies (for example, a portable hard drive in an office where employees normally access data and software via the network) and behavior (an unauthorized employee or vendor asking for confidential data files), just as they would report unattended luggage in an airport departure lounge.

Look out for threats when hiring

It is more critical than ever to use screening processes and interview techniques designed to assess the honesty of potential hires. Examples include criminal background checks, looking for misrepresentations on résumés, and interview questions that directly probe a candidate's moral compass. Our team is developing tests that will allow employers to determine whether prospective employees have dangerous personality traits like those identified by CPNI.

During the interview process you should also assess cybersafety awareness. Does the candidate know what an insider threat is? When might he share passwords with a team member? Under what circumstances might he allow team members to use his computer as himself? If candidates are strong in all other ways, you may go ahead and hire them, but make sure that they are immediately trained in your organization's policies and practices. If someone is being considered for a job in a highly sensitive environment, however, you should think carefully about bringing him or her on board.

Employ rigorous subcontracting processes

As the Target breach demonstrates, you must ensure that your suppliers or distributors don't put you at risk—by, for example, minimizing the likelihood that someone at an external IT provider will create a back door to your systems. If a supplier's risk of failure or a breach is much smaller than yours, it may not adopt the controls you require. Seek out partners and suppliers that have the same risk appetite and culture your organization does, which will make a common approach to cybersecurity much more likely.

Ask potential suppliers during precontractual discussions about how they manage insider-related risk. If you hire them, audit them regularly to see that their practices are genuinely maintained. Make it clear that you will conduct audits, and stipulate what they will involve. A company might require of suppliers the same controls it uses itself: screening employees for criminal records, checking the truth of job candidates' employment histories, monitoring access to its data and applications for unauthorized activity, and preventing intruders from entering sensitive physical premises.

Monitor employees

Let them know that you can and will observe their cyberactivity to the extent permitted by law. You cannot afford to leave cybersecurity entirely to the experts; you must raise your own day-to-day awareness of what is leaving your systems as well as what is coming in. That means requiring security teams or service providers to produce regular risk assessments, which should include the sources of threats, vulnerable employees and networks, and the possible consequences if a risk becomes a reality. You should also measure risk-mitigation behaviors, such as response times to alerts.

Often routers or firewalls can monitor outgoing channels, but you should make sure that the functionality is activated. If you don't have the equipment to monitor outgoing traffic, buy it. You must also log and monitor other means of exfiltration—USB flash drives and other portable storage media, printouts, and so on—through spot checks or even permanent, airport-style searches of people entering and exiting your buildings. (General Electric and Wipro use these in Bangalore.)

For monitoring to be effective, you must diligently manage the privileges of all employees—including those with the highest levels of access to company systems, who are often the instigators of insider attacks. Prune your list of most privileged users regularly—and then watch the ones who remain to verify that they deserve your trust. Look for insider-threat-detection systems that can predict possibly preventable events as well as find events that have already occurred. Big data can be helpful in linking clues and providing warnings.

Malware-detection software can be useful. Particularly in outsider-insider collaborations, a key initial step is introducing malware into the network. When you find malware, consider that it might be part of an insider attack; an analysis of how the malware is being used may provide clues to the identity and wider objectives of the attacker.

Monitoring to this degree will increase everyone's workload but will pay off by building the resilience of and reducing the risk to your enterprise.

The most effective strategy for defusing the cyberthreat posed by insiders is to use the protective technologies available and fix weak points in them, but focus ultimately on getting all insiders to behave in a way that keeps the company safe. People need to know what behaviors are acceptable or unacceptable. Remind them that protecting the organization also protects their jobs.

Originally published September 2014. Reprint R1409G

Future-Proof Your Climate Strategy

by Joseph E. Aldy and Gianfranco Gianfrate

AS GLOBAL WEATHER BECOMES MORE EXTREME, the threat that climate change poses for companies is no longer theoretical. Businesses are working to protect their assets and supply chains from increasingly severe hurricanes, heat waves, fires, and droughts. More and more companies are figuring such "climate risk" into their calculations, and investors are paying close attention. But there is a related threat that many haven't fully taken in: carbon risk—the impact of climate-change policies on a company's strategy and returns. As global warming worsens, companies can expect tougher government measures that will extract a growing price for their carbon emissions. These mechanisms could sideline the unprepared. In this article we describe the approach used by more and more companies to brace for the future and even flourish in it: internal carbon pricing. (See the exhibit "The rise of internal carbon pricing.") At its core, this involves setting a monetary value on the company's own emissions that reflects carbon prices outside the firm. In 2017 nearly 1,400 companies were actively using internal carbon pricing or planning to do so. As we'll show, by putting their own price on carbon, companies can better evaluate investments, manage risk, and forge strategy.

Before we get into the details, let's consider the context. U.S. companies may think the pressure's off, given the Trump administration's efforts to dismantle existing climate and energy policies. But the rest of the world, and many U.S. states, are plowing ahead to strengthen their efforts to fight climate change. More than 60 regional, national, and subnational governments—representing about half of the global economy—have implemented policies that price carbon emissions, and 184 nations have ratified the Paris Agreement to reduce them. The governments of Mexico, Sweden, British Columbia, and other jurisdictions are currently levying taxes. And China, the European Union, and California are among those rolling out cap-and-trade programs that put a ceiling on total emissions to create incentives for reducing them. (See the sidebar "How Governments Price Carbon.")

Thus even with the policy retreat under way in Washington, DC, American corporations must actively manage the potential increased cost of their emissions if carbon prices rise—for several reasons. First, state-level cap-and-trade programs have already

The rise of internal carbon pricing

The number of global companies that have adopted an ICP is growing rapidly.

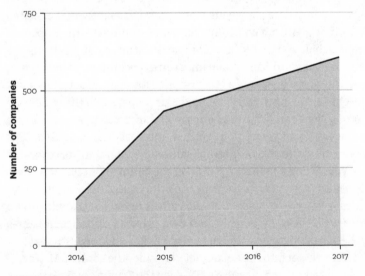

Source: CDP, Putting a Price on Carbon (2017).

Idea in Brief

The Challenge

Companies commonly take into account climate-change threats to their assets and operations. But they are less proactive about considering the risks that climate-change policies pose to their strategy and returns.

The Solution

Predicting that those policies will extract a growing price for firms' carbon emissions, more and more companies are setting a monetary value on their own emissions to help them evaluate investments, manage risk, and develop strategy.

The Process and the Payoff

Companies must forecast future carbon prices in the jurisdictions where they do business and then set an internal carbon price (ICP) that reflects their emissions and the likely trajectory of carbon prices set by governments. A carefully calculated ICP can position a firm for future regulation and help it gain long-term advantage.

---

led to carbon pricing for about one-quarter of the electricity consumed in the United States. Second, federal and state policies—such as regulations pertaining to fuel economy, the energy efficiency of appliances, biofuels, and renewable power—can impose an implicit carbon price on the firms that must comply with those rules. Third, the likelihood of expanded carbon pricing under a future administration and Congress must be considered when making investments in long-lived equipment, factories, and power plants. Finally, many American corporations operate in or sell products to countries that have already implemented cap-and-trade programs or carbon taxes.

It's no wonder that companies are finding it hard to quantify the risk posed by this myriad of policies or to see potential opportunities. And consider how heterogeneous and volatile the policies are. Cap-and-trade emission allowances in the EU Emissions Trading System, for example, were trading at €5 per ton of carbon dioxide in 2017 but jumped to more than €20 per ton in 2018. Those prices apply to some sources of carbon dioxide in Sweden, but others there face a separate carbon tax greater than €90 per ton. And California's emission allowances have traded at prices three times those in the Regional Greenhouse Gas Initiative, a power-sector cap-and-trade program in the Northeast and mid-Atlantic states.

How Governments Price Carbon

GOVERNMENTS HAVE TWO DIRECT MECHANISMS for pricing carbon: a tax on CO_2 emissions and a market-based cap-and-trade scheme. Governments can also indirectly affect carbon pricing by enacting energy regulations that result in compliance costs for companies.

Carbon Tax

A carbon tax is straightforward: A government imposes a tax on each ton of carbon dioxide emitted. But gauging emissions is tricky—it's not easy to measure the CO_2 flowing from the tailpipes of a fleet of trucks, for instance. Therefore, a carbon tax is often applied not to actual emissions but to the carbon content of fossil fuels used, because the complete combustion of a ton of coal, a cubic foot of natural gas, or a barrel of oil produces a known quantity of carbon dioxide.

In the United States, applying a carbon tax could be administratively simple if it piggybacked on existing excise taxes for oil and coal. Refineries and importers of refined petroleum products already pay a tax of nine cents a barrel to finance the Oil Spill Liability Trust Fund, and coal mine operators pay a per-ton tax to support the Black Lung Disability Trust Fund. Imposing a carbon tax on natural-gas processors and importers would cover the balance of fossil fuel companies. Such a scheme would apply to about 98% of U.S. carbon dioxide emissions by covering only a few thousand producers as opposed to the hundreds of millions of smokestacks, tailpipes, and other sources of emissions. And judging from the experiences under similar upstream carbon taxes in British Columbia and Northern Europe, a tax would pass through to energy prices, creating incentives for energy efficiency, conservation, and lower-carbon sources of energy.

Carbon policies may be all over the map, but one thing is virtually certain: In time, every jurisdiction will have some pricing scheme in place. By setting an internal carbon price (ICP), companies can prepare for uncertain external pricing in the future, and investors can get a clearer picture of a firm's ability to compete in a low-carbon world.

Getting Started

Internal carbon pricing allows companies to place a monetary value on emitting a ton of carbon, even when few or none of their operations are currently subject to external carbon-pricing policies

Cap and Trade

A cap-and-trade program starts with the objective of limiting the aggregate quantity of emissions, which is represented by the cap. A government divides this total quantity into "allowances" that permit holders to emit a specific amount of carbon dioxide. These are typically either sold to bidders at an auction or provided free to firms covered by the program, with allocations based on their historical emissions. The covered firms must report their emissions to the government and surrender allowances equal to those emissions. In these programs, firms may buy and sell allowances in a secondary market, and the price that emerges from this trading reflects the cost of reducing a ton of pollution.

Price Implied by Regulation

Government energy policies do not always put an explicit price on carbon; sometimes they merely create implicit prices by imposing compliance costs on companies. The government might, for instance, require that a share of electricity generation come from renewable sources or that an appliance meet a minimum energy-efficiency standard. In such cases, the carbon price isn't determined by a tax or a cap-and-trade program, but individual firms can estimate an implied price by calculating how much they spend to comply with the regulations. Implied prices are less transparent than those determined by a tax or a market for allowances, and they are likely to vary from firm to firm, but they can still inform a company's strategic decisions.

and related regulations. Companies use internal pricing in three key ways: to inform decisions about capital investments (especially when projects directly affect emissions, energy efficiency, or changes in the portfolio of energy sources); to measure, model, and manage the financial and regulatory risks associated with existing and potential government pricing regimes; and to help identify risks and opportunities and adjust strategy accordingly.

Although an ICP may be levied as an actual fee on business units within a company (as we discuss later), it is more typically a theoretical price used in economic and strategic analyses. For some companies, the price adopted internally is just a reflection of the existing carbon tax or price imposed where they do business. Some firms may not have operations in jurisdictions with explicit carbon-pricing policies, but they may still face carbon risk if their supply chains extend into those areas, especially if they are large consumers of electricity, fuels, and energy-intensive manufactured goods.

The prices adopted by companies globally vary widely, with some companies pricing carbon as low as one cent per ton while others assess it at well above $100 per ton. To put those numbers in context, $10 per ton of CO_2 translates into about 10 cents per gallon of gasoline, one cent per kilowatt-hour of electricity from a coal-fired power plant, and 0.5 cents per kilowatt-hour from a natural gas–fired power plant. The carbon price selected depends on the industry, the country, and the company's objectives. (See the exhibit "The range of internal carbon prices.")

Before we illustrate the various ways in which firms use internal carbon pricing, it's important to understand how they determine a carbon price.

Measuring Carbon Footprints

At the outset, companies must get a clear picture of their emissions. Since different countries (and different states in the same country) are adopting different environmental regulations and carbon prices, companies should determine the quantity and geographic location of both their direct and their indirect CO_2 emissions. Energy firms and energy-intensive manufacturers in the United States already report their direct emissions to the U.S. Environmental Protection Agency (EPA) under two separate requirements, but most other companies are further behind in quantifying how much carbon dioxide they're generating.

Direct emissions (often referred to as scope 1 emissions) come from sources owned or controlled by the company—for example, emissions from combustion in a company's boilers or from its vehicle fleet. Indirect scope 2 emissions result from a company's consumption of purchased electricity, heat, steam, and cooling.

The range of internal carbon prices

Some companies price carbon as low as one cent per ton, while others assess it at well above $100 per ton. The price depends on the industry, the country, and the company's objectives. Here's a look at the distribution of 185 firms by price range in 2017.

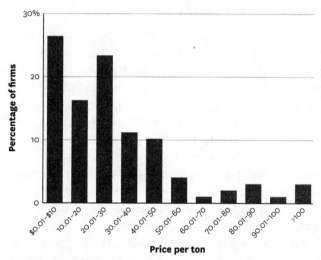

Source: Authors' calculations based on CDP data.

Other indirect emissions (scope 3) occur up and down a company's supply chain—for example, in the production and transport of purchased materials and in waste disposal. The distinction between direct and indirect emissions shows that even companies that aren't in carbon-intensive industries may actually be responsible for significant emissions. The global reinsurer Swiss Re, for instance, has very low direct CO_2 emissions, but in 2017 its indirect emissions from business travel were 15 times as high as its direct emissions per employee. To raise awareness and decrease unnecessary flights, the company applies an internal carbon fee to its business units, charging each for the emissions associated with its employees' trips.

A framework for mapping emissions is beyond the scope of this article, but many resources are publicly available. For example, Greenhouse Gas Protocol has created a standardized approach for measuring and managing corporate emissions, and it provides accounting and reporting standards, guidance by sector, and calculation tools.

Forecasting Future Carbon Prices

After mapping their emissions, companies should examine their exposure to current and estimated future carbon prices, beginning with an assessment of existing climate policies in the countries where they operate or plan to expand. In jurisdictions with cap-and-trade policies, the price placed on a ton of carbon is made explicit in the marketplace for emissions allowances—for example, on the European Energy Exchange platform. In other jurisdictions, carbon tax rates can be easily determined by looking at national tax laws. Additionally, several international organizations have compiled explicit and implicit carbon prices under existing government policies. The World Bank provides updated data from each national regulatory system in its annual *State and Trends of Carbon Pricing.* The OECD has recently published "effective carbon rates" that account for explicit carbon prices (such as EU Emissions Trading System allowance prices) and implicit carbon prices (such as gasoline taxes and regulatory mandates).

Current carbon prices are useful data points, but to build a long-term strategy, companies also need to make predictions about future carbon prices. This is a daunting exercise, given the lack of clear and consistent signals from governments and the uncertainty about technological and economic developments that could affect carbon pricing policies. But a collaborative approach can help.

In 2017 CDP (formerly the Carbon Disclosure Project) and the We Mean Business coalition created the Carbon Pricing Corridors initiative, which engages large companies in identifying industry-specific carbon price levels necessary to achieve the Paris Agreement goals. For example, in the chemical industry (according to executives from companies representing about $200 billion in market capitalization), carbon prices for 2020 should range from $30 to $50 per ton, increasing to $50 to $100 per ton by 2035. These numbers reveal three important insights about the implications of public policy for business. First, companies need to think beyond current regulations; the 2020 range is much higher than the price of carbon currently imposed by climate policies in most countries. Second, the average price is expected to increase over time as more-aggressive climate policies are enacted. Third, the range of prices will widen; the longer the time horizon, the greater the uncertainty about the possible impact of policy and technology innovations.

Predicting carbon prices requires navigating and critically reviewing data and analyses from climate experts, research institutions, peer companies, and environmental agencies. Forecasts produced by academics and government analysts are based on assumptions that are difficult for nonexperts to fully gauge. And relying solely on the estimates disclosed by peer companies may lead to groupthink effects and biased forecasts. Companies need to develop in-house expertise or rely on external professionals to identify the likely evolution of public policies and associated carbon prices. Ideally, they should project not only the level of prices but also the timeline of their changes, the extreme values that could be reached, and the probabilities attached to each possible scenario. (See the sidebar "Carbon Price Scenarios and Simulations.")

Setting Internal Carbon Prices

With a sense of the likely trajectory of external carbon prices, companies can set their ICPs. This requires a deep understanding of both carbon economics and company operations and strategy.

One consideration is the time period that an internal carbon price is expected to cover. It is not uncommon for a company to adopt different prices for decisions with different time horizons. For example, when bidding on contracts, Acciona, a Spanish infrastructure developer, varies its internal price as follows: €36 per ton for near-term projects, €45 per ton for projects that extend through 2030, and €72 per ton for those that will continue through 2050.

In making short- to medium-term decisions, it's probably adequate to set ICPs in line with current carbon prices. That's what Alphabet did in 2016, when it reported to the CDP an internal carbon price of $14 per ton of CO_2—a price aligned with the market value of the allowances traded that year in California's cap-and-trade system. When making business decisions with a long-term impact, such as those that affect a firm's business model, applying an internal price that reflects future scenarios makes more sense. ExxonMobil is highly exposed to enduring carbon risk domestically and internationally; it therefore uses a high ICP of $80 per ton—more than five times Alphabet's and closer to the long-term social cost of carbon used by the EPA, the U.S. Department of Energy, and the U.S. Department of Transportation in many of their regulatory impact analyses over the past decade.

Some companies have established specific emissions or carbon-intensity targets. Carefully considered ICPs can help them meet those targets. In most cases these ICPs are framed as "shadow prices," meaning that the carbon price is included in the evaluation of investment options, just as other costs are. This price, rather than representing actual outlays today, may reflect the costs the firm expects to be imposed on carbon emissions as public policy and regulations evolve over the lifetime of the investment. Suppose a firm is choosing among energy sources for a new power plant. Fossil-based energy may be the cheapest option given current regulations, but when a carbon price reflecting likely future climate policies is taken into account, a renewable power source may be more financially attractive. Similarly, shadow pricing may reveal hidden costs related to an investment. ConocoPhillips reported that after factoring in shadow pricing, it abandoned an investment project that otherwise looked financially worthwhile.

Sometimes internal carbon prices are not just hypothetical costs; as we saw with Swiss Re, they can be used to set and then levy an actual fee on business units for their emissions. The goal is to encourage a shift to low-carbon investments and behaviors, so the ICP must be set high enough to drive the desired change. Companies using this model charge each business unit an amount proportional

Carbon Price Scenarios and Simulations

AN ESSENTIAL PART of setting an internal carbon price is anticipating not only the most likely level of external prices but also the consequences of possible extreme prices. When evaluating carbon risk, managers and investors should consider enhancing their valuation approaches by using models based on scenarios and simulations.

The standard valuation approach is to estimate future cash flows that reflect the cost impact of the most likely future price of carbon. Scenarios allow more-effective valuations than this standard method does. Scenario-based valuation requires at least two but often three scenarios: a best case, a most likely one, and a worst case. The future cash flows under all the scenarios are then estimated, and the various valuation outcomes can be considered as measures of the "value at risk," showing how the investment value will change if extreme carbon prices are hit.

Consider this example: A company evaluates three scenarios. The project value is $100 million under the most likely scenario (a carbon price of $15 per ton), $120 million under the optimistic scenario ($10 per ton), and $40 million under the pessimistic scenario ($25 per ton). That's quite a range: The project could be worth 20% more than the likely value of $100 million, or it could be worth 60% less. But we can better judge the upside potential and the downside risk of the investment by weighting each scenario with the probability that it will occur. In this case, assuming that the most likely scenario has a 50% probability and the other two scenarios each have a 25% probability, we can conclude that the expected value of the project is $90 million [($100 million x 0.5) + ($120 million x 0.25) + ($40 million x 0.25)]. This scenario-based valuation is clearly more informative than one based on a single ICP.

Expanding on this approach, simulation-based valuations focus on the full probability distributions of key variables affecting future cash flows, in lieu of a small set of possible scenarios. Representing the uncertainty over future carbon prices with a probability distribution, company analysts can deliver project valuations that reflect all possible states of the world. This approach is mathematically complex, but it can be easily handled by common software packages such Oracle Crystal Ball.

to the emissions associated with its energy consumption. The fees generated can then be used either to reward the units with the best emissions-reduction performance or to make further investments to green the company. In 2012 Microsoft implemented an internal carbon-pricing system that holds business units accountable for their scope 1, 2, and 3 emissions. The collected fees—ranging from $5 to $10 per ton—are pooled in a central company fund that invests in internal efficiency projects, green energy, and carbon offset programs. Overall, Microsoft has reported more than $10 million in energy cost savings each year and emissions reductions of nearly 10 million tons since 2012.

A final consideration in setting internal carbon prices is an organization's incentives for executives to deliver on carbon-reduction initiatives. If the company has ambitious targets and compensates its managers accordingly against those targets, higher ICPs can be instrumental in achieving objectives.

Applying the Price

Let's look more closely at how companies factor internal carbon prices into their decisions about new investments, risk management, and long-term strategy.

New investments

When evaluating investments, a firm can assess the carbon footprint of each option and use its internal carbon price to estimate the potential carbon costs. For example, when deciding how to source energy for a new plant, an ICP can be applied to estimate the carbon costs of fossil-based electricity versus renewable sources. The product of the internal carbon price and the expected carbon footprint becomes a financial cost included in the net present valuation of the project.

The use of an internal carbon price enhances the quality of the financial valuation by allowing a more informed decision about production costs such as energy, machines, and materials, assigning them an implicit price that is more likely to increase than decrease over time. Beginning in 2016, Michelin set an internal carbon price of €50 per ton. Multiplying this price by a project's expected carbon footprint over its lifetime allows the company to estimate the project's carbon cost and return on investment. In this way, Michelin's executives consider the implied cost of carbon—even for markets where there is currently no regulated carbon price—as they make decisions about production capacity increases, boiler upgrades, and logistics. Michelin intentionally set an ICP higher than the carbon price imposed in Europe and China, with the objective of getting its operations climate-ready both in countries with no climate regulations and in those where existing rules are likely to become more stringent.

Risk management

Climate policies are changing fast, and the regulated prices of carbon can move abruptly. Internal carbon prices are useful for gauging the impact of regulatory changes and assessing exposure to carbon risk throughout the supply chain, beyond the operations directly controlled by the company. Managing carbon risk is similar to managing other financial risks (such as currency and interest rate fluctuations) and compliance risks.

In jurisdictions that have cap-and-trade systems, power plants and factories must pay for allowances that grant them the right to emit carbon. Higher carbon prices make it more expensive for utilities to burn fossil fuels, thus encouraging a shift to cleaner sources of power. Utilities are hedging their exposure to rising carbon prices through energy investment decisions and carbon-allowance transactions, including the purchase and banking of allowances for use in the future, when allowance prices are expected to be higher. Internal carbon prices provide guidance for the hedging strategies of many utilities.

ICPs are also instrumental in managing regulatory compliance. Teck Resources, a Canadian metals and mining company, systematically conducts analyses to better understand firm exposure and risks under various carbon-pricing and regulatory scenarios. For example, in evaluating the exposure of its operations in British Columbia, it uses a variety of scenarios that assume ICPs ranging from $30 per ton (matching the provincial government's current tax) to $50 per ton (the planned tax for 2021). Such scenarios have allowed the company to estimate potential carbon costs in 2022 that will range from $45 million to $80 million—valuable information that informs Teck Resources' financial planning. Importantly, carbon risk management should not be limited to firms' operations; internal carbon pricing can allow firms to reduce carbon risk up and down their supply chains by helping them benchmark suppliers and design carbon-reducing collaborations with them.

Strategy

Internal carbon pricing can inform long-term strategy that accelerates emissions reduction and helps companies find new markets and revenue opportunities. The Swedish packaging and processing company Tetra Pak, for example, has used its ICP in new-product development. Tetra Pak sets its ICP dynamically using the EU Emissions Trading System price as a reference point, with a floor price of €10 per ton. Such pricing helped the company gauge the potential financial impact of incorporating recycled and renewable materials into caps, cartons, and other packaging products, and it supported the introduction of more renewables into the company's supply chain. It has also helped Tetra Pak launch innovative new packaging that uses less aluminum, which is energy-intensive to produce. Goldman Sachs has adopted an internal carbon price to help it achieve carbon neutrality in its operations. More broadly, its sophisticated understanding of carbon economics and scenario planning has allowed it to become the major financier for clean-energy companies globally and a leading underwriter for new products such as green bonds.

Assessing Results and Engaging Stakeholders

The integration of carbon prices into operations and strategic decisions should be regularly reassessed and the results fed back into the process to set updated prices. For example, if the ICP isn't driving enough emissions reduction by the business units, or if the firm operates in a jurisdiction where the carbon price is higher than the firm's ICP, it might make sense to raise the internal price.

Getting the business carbon-ready requires real commitment and a cultural transformation that should start with the board and top management. Leadership must communicate the firm's emissions targets and strategies to all employees and consider monetary incentives for delivering on the targets. Companies should share the objectives of their ICP programs with partners along the supply chain and work with suppliers and customers to reduce their carbon risk. This will help optimize the ICP and enhance collaboration with all stakeholders—including customers, supply chain partners, local communities where green funds are directed, and, crucially, investors.

Investors have become increasingly eager to understand how firms manage the risks and opportunities under climate-change policies. For example, BlackRock, the world's largest asset manager, recently announced plans to press companies to disclose how climate change could affect their business. And in 2017, more than 60% of ExxonMobil's shareholders approved a resolution calling for greater disclosure of the financial risks posed by long-term climate-change policy.

Scenario-planning techniques, coupled with rigorous analysis of climate-policy risks, can provide executives with a broad view of how their business might evolve under various carbon-pricing regimes. Developing these sophisticated capabilities can help managers engage more effectively with regulators and policy makers.

Getting on Board

Many companies don't yet price carbon. Some may be fairly carbon-lean and thus don't expect emerging carbon policies to have a significant impact on their cash flows. This is often a false assumption. Companies with negligible scope 1 emissions may still be high polluters when scope 2 and 3 emissions are considered. Other firms aren't pricing carbon because they lack the capabilities needed to anticipate and evaluate potential regulations and policies, and they don't fully realize how exposed they are to carbon risk.

However, the rapid adoption of internal carbon pricing shows that companies increasingly recognize its importance to competitive operations and strategy. Only firms that understand and proactively manage carbon risk will sustain long-term advantage as more and more countries move to decarbonize their economies.

Originally published May–June 2019. Reprint R1903E

About the Contributors

JOSEPH E. ALDY is a professor of public policy at Harvard Kennedy School.

SADIE CREESE is the professor of cybersecurity at Oxford. She is a principal investigator in the Corporate Insider Threat Detection research program.

GEORGE S. DAY is the Geoffrey T. Boisi Professor at the Wharton School, a codirector of the Mack Institute for Innovation Management, and a former executive director of the Marketing Science Institute.

MATTHEW J. EYRING is the managing partner of the strategy and innovation consulting firm Innosight.

GIANFRANCO GIANFRATE is an associate professor of finance at EDHEC Business School.

CLARK G. GILBERT is the CEO of Deseret News Publishing and Deseret Digital Media.

KARAN GIROTRA is a professor at INSEAD in Fontainebleau, France, and a coauthor, with Serguei Netessine, of *The Risk-Driven Business Model: Four Questions That Will Define Your Company* (Harvard Business Review Press, 2014).

DANIEL G. GOLDSTEIN is a principal research scientist at Microsoft Research.

PAUL HEALY is the James R. Williston Professor of Business Administration at Harvard Business School.

ROBERT S. KAPLAN is a senior fellow and the Marvin Bower Professor of Leadership Development, Emeritus, at Harvard Business School.

ANETTE MIKES is an associate professor of accounting at the University of Oxford's Saïd Business School.

SERGUEI NETESSINE is the Vice Dean for Global Initiatives and the Dhirubhai Ambani Professor of Innovation and Entrepreneurship at the University of Pennsylvania's Wharton School and a coauthor, with Karan Girotra, of *The Risk-Driven Business Model: Four Questions That Will Define Your Company* (Harvard Business Review Press, 2014).

CONDOLEEZZA RICE is a professor of political economy at the Stanford Graduate School of Business, a senior fellow at the Hoover Institution, and a professor of political science at Stanford University. She served as national security adviser from 2001 to 2005 and as the 66th US secretary of state from 2005 to 2009. She is the coauthor of *Political Risk: How Businesses and Organizations Can Anticipate Global Insecurity* (Twelve, 2018).

WILLIAM SCHMIDT is an assistant professor at Cornell University's Johnson Graduate School of Management.

PAUL J. H. SCHOEMAKER is the former research director of the Wharton School's Mack Institute and a coauthor of *Peripheral Vision* (Harvard Business Review Press, 2006). He served as an adviser to the Good Judgment Project.

GEORGE SERAFEIM is a professor of business administration at Harvard Business School, a cofounder of KKS Advisors, and the chairman of Greece's National Corporate Governance Council.

DAVID SIMCHI-LEVI is a professor of engineering at the Massachusetts Institute of Technology. He cofounded LogicTools, a provider of software for optimizing supply chains that is now part of IBM; OPS Rules, an operations consulting company; and Opalytics, a cloud analytics platform company. His latest book is *Operations Rules: Delivering Customer Value through Flexible Operations* (MIT Press, 2010).

EUGENE SOLTES is the Jakurski Family Associate Professor of Business Administration at Harvard Business School, where his research focuses on corporate misconduct.

MARK W. SPITZNAGEL is a principal of Universa Investments.

NASSIM N. TALEB is the Distinguished Professor of Risk Engineering at New York University's Tandon School of Engineering and a principal of Universa Investments. He is the author of several books, including *The Black Swan: The Impact of the Highly Improbable* (Random House, 2007).

PHILIP E. TETLOCK is the Leonore Annenberg University Professor of Psychology and Management at the University of Pennsylvania and a coauthor of *Superforecasting* (Crown, 2015). He co-led the Good Judgment Project.

DAVID M. UPTON is the American Standard Companies Professor of Operations Management at the University of Oxford's Saïd Business School.

YEHUA WEI is an assistant professor at Duke University's Fuqua School of Business.

AMY ZEGART is codirector of and a senior fellow at Stanford University's Center for International Security and Cooperation, a senior fellow at the Hoover Institution, and a former McKinsey & Company management consultant. She is the coauthor of *Political Risk: How Businesses and Organizations Can Anticipate Global Insecurity* (Twelve, 2018).

Index

Engage with HBR content the way you want, on any device.

With HBR's new subscription plans, you can access world-renowned **case studies** from Harvard Business School and receive **four free eBooks**. Download and customize prebuilt **slide decks and graphics** from our **Visual Library**. With HBR's archive, top 50 best-selling articles, and five new articles every day, HBR is more than just a magazine.

Subscribe Today
hbr.org/success